Ethnicity, Class, Gender and Migration

Greek-Cypriots in Britain

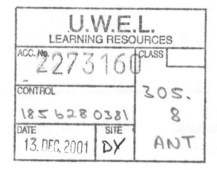
FLOYA ANTHIAS

Avebury

Aldershot · Brookfield USA · Hong Kong · Singapore · Sydney

Published by
Avebury
Ashgate Publishing Ltd
Gower House
Croft Road
Aldershot
Hants GU11 3HR
England

Ashgate Publishsing Company
Old Post Road
Brookfield
Vermont 05036
USA

A CIP catalogue record for this book is available from the British Library and the US Library of Congress.

ISBN 1 85628 038 1

Printed and Bound in Great Britain by
Athenaeum Press Ltd., Newcastle upon Tyne.

UNIVERSITY OF WOLVERHAMPTON
Harrison Learning Centre

ITEMS ISSUED:

Customer ID: WPP61343935

Title: British immigration policy since 1939 : the
making of multi-racial Britain
ID: 7621421609
Due: 13/04/2017 23:59

Title: myth of return : Pakistanis in Britain
ID: 7606125131
Due: 13/04/2017 23:59

Title: Ethnicity, class, gender and migration .
Greek-Cypriots in Britain
ID: 7622731601
Due: 13/04/2017 23:59

Title: Migration and race relations in an English
city : a study in Bristol; (by) A
ID: 7612614289
Due: 13/04/2017 23:59

Total items: 4
23/03/2017 15:05
Issued: 7
Overdue: 0

Thank you for using Self Service.
Please keep your receipt.

Overdue books are fined at 40p per day for
1 week loans, 10p per day for long loans.

ETHNICITY, CLASS, GENDER AND MIGRATION

Contents

Preface

This book sets out to place Cypriot migration to Britain within the context of New Commonwealth migration and within current developments in the field of 'race' and ethnic studies. It provides an account of the economic and social position of Cypriots in British society paying particular attention to a number of central theoretical and political debates relating to class, ethnicity, cultural identity, racism, gender and generation. The position taken in the book is that ethnic and migrant groups should be understood in terms of the interaction between the internal cultural and social differences and the wider structural and ideological processes of the country of residence. The intersection of ethnic, gender and class divisions is treated as central in this process. In addition the book raises questions about ethnic and racial disadvantage and exclusion. The concrete analysis will focus mainly on Greek-Cypriots although much of the analysis is also applicable to Turkish Cypriots. This is the main reason why at times the term Cypriot rather than Greek-Cypriot is used in the text. Greek-Cypriots are a settler population in Britain who formed part of the phase of New Commonwealth migration during the 'long Boom' of the British Economy in the 1950s and 1960s. There is very little published work that provides an analysis of this experience. This book provides an analytical study of Greek Cypriots in Britain and does not purport to be a systematic empirical study.

The most important method used was that of participant observation. This was the most appropriate for addressing the themes described above. I have extensive knowledge and experience of Greek-Cypriots in Britain. I migrated to England with my parents when I was three years old and was brought up within the Greek Cypriot community in London in a Greek-Cypriot idiom. I have a long association and extensive experience and knowledge of a large number of Greek-Cypriot groups, organisations and individuals. The advantages gained as an 'insider', (such as having established contacts and trust) are well recognised. However, one disadvantage may be that of taking for granted what an outsider may note more carefully. However, this may have been softened by the value relevancies of the study and by a distancing through integration into British society and a sociological background. I do not claim any privileged access, however, for any analysis has to be evaluated from the point of view of the problematic it addresses.

In order to systematise the participant observation, I took extensive field notes of meetings, gatherings and conversations. I have systematically read the Greek–Cypriot press in Cyprus and London and been involved in a large number of associations and events. A large bulk of the field work was conducted between 1980 and 1982 and subsequently 1988–1990.

In addition to participant observation, I conducted a series of structured and unstructured interviews with leaders and representatives of the community and some formal interviewing took place of ordinary Cypriots from a range of occupational, gender and age categories. Many Cypriots are defensive, however, either on their best behaviour or resist probing or intrusive questioning. In such cases notes were made after the visit. Researchers are often treated with suspicion and I usually visited in a social context, facilitated by prior contact with individuals or used family contacts and neighbours. My long standing involvement in the community was an important resource that I drew upon.

In addition to participant observation and interviewing, I made case studies of 44 individuals which helped greatly in building up a picture (see Appendix I).

This study does not make claims to a statistically yielding analysis. A fully fledged survey which would yield statistically significant results, even within the confines of systematic empiricism, was ruled out. I have instead used and done my own calculations with published official data, especially the 1971 and to a lesser extent the 1981 Census of Populations (see Appendix II) and data collected by other surveyors and researchers where possible. An additional research tool was the content analysis of two Greek Cypriot papers, Vema (which is now extinct) and Parikiaki, with particular focus on articles and perspectives on the community.

The book is aimed at a general audience that is interested in issues of race and ethnicity, as well as undergraduates and postgraduates. I hope that it will be of use to teachers, policy makers and community workers in areas where there is a large Cypriot population. Finally but not least, it has been written for the 200,000 Cypriot population in Britain, a population I grew up amongst, and have many bonds with. It is dedicated to my parents Anastasia and Tefcros Anthias, whose own active participation and involvement in the Cypriot community provided the most central incentive for the book, and to my brother Tefcros, and sister Andry, who shared with me the experience of growing up in a Greek Cypriot family and culture in British society.

Chapter 1 introduces the main parameters within which the book is located, and provides an overview of the migration and settlement of Cypriots to Britain. In Chapter 2 current issues in the sociology of ethnicity and race are examined, and the theoretical framework of the book developed. Chapter 3 contextualises Greek–Cypriots in economic and ethnic relations in Cyprus. Chapter 4 examines issues of exclusion and opportunity by looking at employment, housing and education in order to assess the extent and nature of ethnic and class disadvantage. In Chapters

5 and 6 the question of the links between gender and ethnic divisions is examined. Chapter 7 considers the issue of cultural identity, generational divisions, British Cypriot culture and the politics of ethnicity. Finally, Chapter 8 concludes the argument of the book by setting out the location of Cypriots within ethnic and race processes in Britain.

1 The migration and settlement of Greek-Cypriots in Britain

Introduction

Greek–Cypriots [1] formed part of the phase of New Commonwealth migration during the 'long boom' of the British economy in the 1950s and 1960s. The aim of this book is to provide an analysis of a settler population from a colonial region in the light of central theoretical and political debates relating to ethnicity, class, gender and cultural identity. The structures of ethnic exclusion and disadvantage, and the links between class, ethnic and gender processes are pivotal themes of the book. The analysis problematises the notion of ethnicity. This is neither a unitary category nor can it be considered outside wider questions of collectivity and the way this is attributed and proclaimed. Nor can these questions be analysed without considering the links between ethnic, class and gender divisions. Ethnicity is dynamically and situationally constituted and has heterogeneous relevance for different ethnic groups and the economic, sexual and generational categories within them.

Greek–Cypriots present a useful case study for exploring these issues. Studies of ethnic minorities in Britain have tended to be dominated by a race relations problematic which focuses on the effects of racialisation and racism on the economic and social position of an ethnic group, or on the extent to which cultural and structural assimilation or integration takes place. Greek Cypriots are not generally regarded as a racialised category, and are usually left out of those discussions whose focus is racial prejudice or institutionalised racism. Greek Cypriots are however colonial migrants and much of the literature within what can be termed 'the race relations problematic' (Miles, 1982) has sought to link the origins of racism within capitalism to the historical development of colonialist relations. If it is the material relations of colonialism that are implicated it clearly cannot be argued that there is a separate sphere of 'Black' colonial relations that merely relates to the ascriptive characteristic of skin colour.

In addition as colonial migrants from an underdeveloped region, Cypriots brought with them cultural visibility, low language skills, low occupational and educational qualifications and non- initiation into the structural openings and cultural capital of British social relations. They arc also a physically visible minority group particularly in certain areas of high concentration in London. But more importantly perhaps, ethnic disadvantage is implicated in structures of employment, housing and access to the state in interplay with the ethnic and class resources of the group. Ethnic disadvantage is linked moreover to exclusion processes structured by the sectarianism and dominant ethnicity of British society both at the institutional level and that of the employer and working class. The distinction between racial and ethnic categories is therefore raised. The independent effectivity of racial ideologies in structuring class disadvantage and the economic incorporation of migrant or ethnic minority groups is also an issue.

Greek–Cypriot men and women were 'migrant labour' like other New Commonwealth migrants. Theories of the role of migrant labour within the capitalist mode of production were developed with particular reference to the Western European experience. Attempts have been made to consider the British case in this light. The forms of economic incorporation of Greek–Cypriots must also be included if any such analysis is to be attempted. Clearly if migrant labour is considered to have a function for capitalism at the centre (as many of these analyses claim) then this function cannot be limited to groups that share particular ascriptive characteristics, such as black skins (for just such an analysis see Phizacklea and Miles, 1980). The Cypriot case can highlight the problems of applying the notion of migrant labour, as a unitary category, to the British case.

Economic participation and employment characteristics have often been attributed to the exercise of particular cultural choices by members of ethnic groups. This explanation is used at times to account for differences between groups where racism and its effects cannot be used or as an alterative explanation. Although questions of culture, and cultural maintenance, identity and language are important (and indeed becoming increasingly so), cultural idioms are neither statically given nor are they merely voluntaristically constituted. Questions of cultural identity and affirmation are political questions for ethnic groups and activity around these does not merely denote an ideological or natural identification with the culture of origin. Such activity may be centrally informed by economic, political and strategic considerations. Here clearly issues of class position of the group become important, for what may appear as ethnic behaviour may be expressive of economic or political positioning and the working class urban industrial complex of relations that the group shares. Cultural choices and identities therefore need to be examined within the context of migrant or ethnic exclusion and disadvantage.

What is particularly marked for Cypriots is the continuation of the salience of the ethnic category and the development of an ethnic economy which provides both employment and services for many Cypriots. Cypriots have a low assimilation rate into British culture both economically and socially. Although this is not primarily the result of direct forms of racist exclusion which certainly exist (Swann, 1985), nonetheless the analysis in this book indicates that it cannot be understood only with reference to

2

cultural identity or the choices made by ethnic subjects. Greek–Cypriot ethnicity is not confined to the arena of distinct cultural idioms and identities, but is expressed in a highly organised community structure with its own political, social and educational organisations. The extent to which ethnicity can be used as a resource in the management of ethnic disadvantage and its class implications is an issue here.

There are three elements at least that have to be taken into account In explaining the economic and social positioning of Cypriots in Britain that relate to the country of origin and the form that migration took. One is the form of Greek–Cypriot ethnicity which developed in the post war period and is linked to the growth of nationalist politics and anti–British/anticolonial sentiments. This focuses the orientation of Greek–Cypriots on Cyprus itself, constructed as a martyred motherland, and provided a romantic and at times passionate attachment to the struggles of the Cypriot people, amplified by the continuing ramifications of the Cyprus problem.

A further factor is the marked extent to which migration took an economic character. Most Cypriots in the post war period came to Britain from the depopulating rural areas, some having already migrated to the towns to find work, in order to improve their material position and escape the poverty and uncertainty of Cypriot life. They also responded to the economic boom (the "long boom" as it has been called) in the 1950s and 1960s in Britain. Many Greek–Cypriots came with a view to returning to Cyprus eventually and although the majority of Greek Cypriots have become permanent settlers the behaviour of the first generation cannot be understood fully without taking into account the 'ideology of return'. This ideology also affects, although to a lesser extent, the British born Cypriots. This imaginary return to the origin affects their participation within Britain and reinforces ethnic social values and networks (that is not to say that these do not become transformed, however, within the British context).

Finally, the traditional Greek–Cypriot family and gender divisions are central in constructing the form of Greek–Cypriot identification and positioning in Britain. Women are both transmitters of the 'cultural stuff' of ethnicity and are its bearers. The traditional skills of women, like sewing and cooking, facilitated the development of an ethnic economy based in clothing, catering and retailing (Anthias, 1983). Indeed an important argument of this study is that Greek–Cypriot female labour, as family and cheap labour, was the cornerstone of the ethnic economy and that it has been crucial, in many cases, in the achievement of the economistic aims of migration.

The Migration and Settlement of Greek-Cypriots in Britain

Migration from the less developed world to the developed world has often meant the transference of population from the colonial periphery to its metropolitan centre. This migration has been seen either as a search by colonial migrants for an improved economic position or by their colonial masters for a profit making labour force. While both of these explanations are adequate in describing the motives for migration and its consequences at the empirical level, migration is not simply linked to immediate economic motives or interests (Castells, 1975). What must surely always be asked is how material conditions are structured within the colony in order for migration to appear such an attractive proposition or indeed the only solution to the unsatisfactory economic circumstances experienced.

The conditions conducive to migration from Cyprus developed within a colonialist context and a primarily agricultural economy with chronic underemployment and land fragmentation. The failure of the colonial government in Cyprus to provide sufficient resources and personnel for the mechanisation of agriculture, and the concomitant failure to encourage sufficiently local industrial development, are important factors in spurring the Cypriot to seek material improvement elsewhere.

In Britain economic conditions in the post war period brought full employment and a growth in labour demand. This was the period in Britain of colonial migration and workers from the New Commonwealth flooded into Britain as replacement workers for the jobs that the indigenous population vacated for more lucrative and stable employment.

Cypriots who migrated tended to choose England or Australia with England being preferred during the 1950s. The choice of England was linked to a variety of factors including familiarity with the colonial power, the economic situation in Britain and the establishment of an early settlement of Cypriots in the 1930s. The demand for labour in Britain gave rise to reports that 'the streets were paved with gold'. Each village had someone who had already 'made good' in catering or a small business and who was willing to sponsor a relative or friend. The lifting of affidavit restrictions in 1954 is of central relevance here (Oakley, 1979). An already established small community existed with its newspaper, organisations and a flow of information was thus generated. A social network of friends and relations in London could help the migrant to find work and accommodation.

Post war developments in Britain had an important role to play as they coincided with the growth of urbanism in Cyprus, the political instability in the wake of the 'national' struggle with the guerilla warfare of EOKA (Anthias and Ayres, 1983), and the economic effects these had. Britain was experiencing an economic boom at the same time as Cyprus was moving into a sphere of greater political uncertainty and urban migration.

The 'long boom' of the early 1950s to the late 1960s in Britain brought a growth of reformism and the welfare state, and changes in occupational structure, that entailed many workers moving into white collar employment. These were linked to the expanding economy and the need for sources of unskilled or semi skilled labour (or replacement labour (Rex, 1970)) in British industry. In the years 1951–1961 those who came from the New Commonwealth more than doubled to 541,000 (Castles and Kosack, 1973:31). The relationship between labour demand and immigration has been demonstrated by Ceri Peach (1968). Legal changes and social policy also helped to produce a spate of migration before the gates ware closed (sic) effectively with the Commonwealth Immigrants Act of 1962.

Immigration to Britain can be divided into three periods, the Jewish (1870–1911), the Irish (1800–1861), and the Commonwealth (1950–1971). The latter can be divided into the periods before and after the Commonwealth Immigrants Act of 1962. The period between June 1948 and June 1962 are the years of Colonial (New Commonwealth) right to British entry. There is difficulty in estimating the precise numbers from the Census Reports which include children born abroad to British nationals and exclude children born in Britain to immigrant parents. The 1971 Census attempted to correct this by having the parents' country of birth included.

The 1951 Census gives a figure of 1.6 million people who were born outside the U.K. of whom 0.2 million were born in the New Commonwealth. In 1971 the figure had risen to 3 million for those born outside the UK and 1.2 born in the New Commonwealth. The 1981 Census gives a figure of 84,327 for those born in Cyprus and the population of Cypriot origin in Britain is near the 200,000 mark at present (2).

The Commonwealth Immigrants Act of 1962 created three categories of employment vouchers: Voucher A for those with specific jobs to come to, Voucher B for those with specific marketable skills and voucher C for unskilled workers without a job. This last was discontinued in 1965. A series of Immigration Acts since then has effectively 'slammed the door' (Runnymede Trust 1980: Chapter 20) to all New Commonwealth Immigrants with only dependents allowed. The Acts have incorporated within them new definitions of nationality status, with such terms as 'patrial' (1971) and more limitations to citizenship being specified by the New Nationality Bill of 1981 (WING, 1985).

All Commonwealth immigration is characterised by being economically motivated (the Cypriots are no exception) and was built up predominantly in areas where unskilled labour supply was shortest. It tended towards areas where housing was cheapest, like run–down urban centres or transitional zones as Rex and Moore (1967) called them. Residence and work may not be the effects of the cultural preferences of migrants but rather of being forced to live near work or where housing is cheap. However, ethnic concentration may also help in the management of ethnic disadvantage.

The early migrants moved into 'twilight' inner areas abandoned by the indigenous population, and later migrants tended towards those areas where the earlier migrants had settled. In the case of Cypriots it was Soho,

Holborn, Islington and Camden Town in London. By the 1970s, Cypriots tended to move further out into Haringey and Enfield, north of the river.

There are three distinct phases of Cypriot migration:

(a) The interwar period, particularly the 1930s.
(b) The post war period up to 1962.
(c) The period around 1974 with the inflow of refugees after the Turkish invasion of the island.

The bulk of migration took place in the post war period as was the case for other new Commonwealth migration. In the case of Cypriots, unlike other Commonwealth immigrants, official control of immigration began a long time before 1962 and was in operation during the whole of the interwar and post war period, until the 1950s.

By the early 1930s, there were 10,000 Cypriots in Britain, mainly single men employed as waiters in hotel and catering. It is clear that they were thought a problem group. Booth (New Survey of London Life and Labour, 1930) says:

> At the present time the operation of the Aliens Immigration Act has produced an appreciable immigration of low class Cypriots who are technically British subjects. These persons... are content to perform the lowest duties at the lowest wage, and tend to live in Soho. Any considerable increase in their numbers may provide a problem for the industry if not the police (:222).

In the early 1930s the Cyprus Colonial government, with the approval of the Colonial Office, began a system of affidavits of support. Cypriots intending to migrate to the UK had to satisfy the Cyprus Colonial Government that they had a guarantor in the UK who was willing and able to offer them accommodation, employment (or help in finding it) and financial assistance if necessary. Guarantors in the UK signed affidavits of support at the London Office of the Cyprus government after strict enquiries were made. These restrictions were lifted in 1954 just before the outbreak of the Cyprus EOKA activities in 1955. The lifting of the restrictions encouraged migration and there is some evidence that the British sought to diffuse the anti-colonial struggle by facilitating migration (Solomos, forthcoming).

By 1966 there were 100,000 Cypriots in Britain (both Greek and Turkish), about three quarters of whom had settled in London. In fact the bulk of migration took place during the 1950s and early 1960s with the peak years being 1960 and 1961 when Cyprus became an Independent Republic. The Commonwealth Act of 1962 curbed migration with the introduction of the voucher system. A further 12,000 or so came in 1974 as refugees, of whom approximately 2–3,000 remain.

The 1981 Census gives a figure of 84,327 for people born in Cyprus. Estimates of those of Cypriot origin in Britain vary between 160,000 and 200,000, at least three quarters of whom are Greek–Cypriot, the remainder being Turkish–Cypriot. Given that the population of Cyprus in 1974 was only 641,000, Cypriots in Britain constitute a significant proportion of Cypriots. In fact it has been estimated that as many Cypriots live outside Cyprus as within it. London is the largest centre of Cypriot migration with 58,453 people born in Cyprus living in Greater London according to the 1981 Census.

The younger age groups constituted the bulk of those who migrated with the largest groups being those in the 15–19 and 20–24 categories. Only 9 per cent were 50 years old or more. Children and particularly elderly people were under represented. The bulk of actual migrants are now well into middle age with British born children and grandchildren of their own. About two thirds of women and just less than one half of men were already married (Oakley, 1979). Initially many of these married men came to Britain on their own, with their wives joining them generally after a year or two when they had found a place to live and a job. There has always been a tendency for established migrants to bring over their elderly parents, particularly widowed mothers. There was also a tendency, up to the early 1960s, to bring brides over from Cyprus using the arranged marriage system which is called 'proxenia'.

The importance of kinship, the family and village networks is evident in the migration process. The nuclear family form is predominant in Cyprus, albeit with the existence of a strong kinship system. In London in 1966 about one fifth of Cypriot households were composed of six or more people. In the same year over two thirds of Cypriots in London were living in extended family units, usually with a widowed mother or unmarried brothers of or sisters (Oakley, 1971). Multiple households were common in the very earliest stages of migration.

Most migration came from the rural and urban unemployed populations with economic motives being predominant. Cypriot migrants who came in the period 1960–1966 had the following occupational characteristics: 49 per cent were craftsmen, production process workers and labourers and a further 12.5 per cent were Service workers (Oakley, 1971). The majority were from rural origin and had been forced to migrate to the towns because of the depletion of agriculture, chronic underemployment and the forced sales of property via the 'demoprasia' (see Chapter 3). There was instability however in the urban labour market in Cyprus with high unemployment and very low profit margins for craftsmen. This situation spurred the Cypriot to seek material improvement by emigrating, primarily to Britain, during this period.

In addition, the dowry system led many poorer workers who could not 'establish' their daughters to migrate. Girls in the 1960s were often sent from the poorer families in the villages at a very young age to work, save for their dowry and find a marriage partner within the immigrant community. In Cyprus there was a demographic imbalance of the sexes in favour of men (Loizos, 1976). In London, on the other hand there were more Cypriot men than women. Many single women from poorer families came to Britain to improve their life chances which were minimal in the Cyprus context. Female migration from Cyprus needs to be seen as a form of labour migration which was also linked to the material relations of the dowry, of marriage, and the family. These constitute important economic as well as personal and social relations. Women therefore did not come to Britain only as dependents.

Most Cypriot villages have migrants in Britain and the economic and social bonds are maintained through travel, property investment, patronage of new migrants (or more recently refugees) and help in the education of kin or co-villagers in Britain.

Ethnic Settlement and Concentration

Most Cypriots are concentrated in Greater London. The Census Report in 1981 shows that there are 58,453 people born in Cyprus living in Greater London. If we compare the settlement of Cypriots within London over the five Census dates of 1931, 1951, 1961, 1971 and 1981, we find a great shift northwards from central areas of London. Early settlement tended to be in the St. Pancras and Holborn areas with 34.5 per cent and 17 per cent respectively in 1931. In 1951, St Pancras still had 31 per cent of Cypriots with Islington now having 14.8 per cent. In 1961 Islington had 34.7 per cent and St Pancras now had only 15.6 per cent. In 1971 the largest Cypriot born population was concentrated in Haringey with 22.3 per cent followed by Islington with 13.7 per cent. In 1981, Haringey was followed by Enfield.

English towns with the largest Cypriot born population in 1971 were: Birmingham (1030), Manchester (490), Bristol (375), Liverpool (345). English counties with a sizeable population were Lancashire (1920), Warwickshire (1570), Yorkshire, West Riding (1115) and Hampshire (1045). In 1981, the Outer South East had 3794 persons born in Cyprus, the West Midlands had 5521, the South West 3168, the North West had 2513, Yorkshire and Humberside had 2099, East Anglia 1667 and Manchester 1254, This indicates a greater tendency for Cypriots to disperse and venture further afield over time.

The London boroughs with a population of around 2,000 or more are as follows, with comparative figures for 1971 and 1981:

London Borough	1971	1981
Haringey	11,865	11,671
Islington	7,300	4,643
Enfield	4,020	9,240
Hackney	3,985	4,067
Southwark	3,310	3,238
Camden	2,850	1,837
Barnet	2,640	3,906
Lambeth	2,265	1,871
Lewisham	–	2,136

Within London, Cypriot settlement tends to be fairly concentrated north of the river with a tendency to move ever more northwards into the outer London suburbs. Concentration also takes place within boroughs. Within Haringey, for example, Cypriots are most concentrated in the Central

Southern Area. Turnpike Lane has a more than 20 per cent Cypriot population, Green Lanes has a 15–19 per cent and West Green and South Hornsey have a 10–14 per cent population of Cypriots. Those areas with less than 5 per cent Cypriots are the primarily middle class areas of Muswell Hill, Crouch End and Highgate (Figures based on 1971 Census).

Greek–Cypriots are an example of 'economic' migration which has established an ecological base. Such a base facilitates the continuation of the salience of ethnicity since it provides a social framework within which the ethnic dimension can function with little requirement for social interaction with British society. Of course Cypriots cannot and do not lead a totally independent existence for they rely for services and for wider conditions on the British State.

There are two central contributing factors to ethnic separatism however in addition to geographical distribution. Firstly, and very importantly is the development of an ethnic economy, that is a distinct Cypriot idiom of economic life, which shares certain characteristics of entrepreneurship and local supply of goods and labour with other ethnic minorities, especially Asians. Cypriot small shops dominate certain areas of Haringey and Cypriot clothing factories are the staple of the North London Clothing Industry.

Secondly ethnicity is articulated and fostered through the proliferation of ethnic organisations and practices: Greek–Cypriot newspapers and the Greek London radio, political groups, the Wood Green Cypriot Community Centre, advisory centres, Theatro Technis (the Cypriot Theatre group that also provides other services to the community), cultural organisations, voluntary associations, pressure groups, mother tongue classes and a Cypriot educational body, and a whole series of clubs and associations ranging from youth clubs to the Thalassaemia society (see Chapter 7).

Having introduced some central features of Cypriot migration and settlement, I shall now provide the theoretical framework within which the study is located, by considering some current issues in the sociology of ethnicity and race.

Notes

1. The term Greek Cypriot is used in much of the text although the term Cypriot is used when the analysis or material warrants including Turkish and other Cypriots. Turkish Cypriots share many of the experiences of migration, settlement and positioning in Britain with Greek Cypriots and much of the general analysis in the book can therefore also be applied to them.

2 Current issues in the sociology of ethnicity and race

Introduction

The most dominant approach to the study of ethnic minorities in Britain focuses on the relations between ethnic groups. It is possible to distinguish between, on the one hand an ethnic studies and on the other hand a race relations problematic. The problematic of the ethnic studies tradition is that of interaction between distinct cultural groups and its effects (Watson, 1977, Jeffery, 1976, Saifullah-Khan, 1979, Wallman, 1979, Bhachu, 1985). Race/racism or racial prejudice/discrimination are considered complicating variables with regard to questions of cultural maintenance, adaptation or progress of an ethnic minority. Often it is argued that these processes differ for white and black groups given the special disadvantages accruing from colour visibility, racial stigmatisation or 'Black' categorisation which generally means a slower progress towards assimilation or integration for black groups and indeed a possible backlash through the development of resurgent or emergent ethnicity. Within American sociology, this tendency finds expression in the enormously influential debate around social assimilation processes which may or may not be seen to exclude black groupings (Glazer and Moynihan, 1965, 1975).

The race relations tradition, on the other hand, is more centrally concerned with racialised categories, generally defined with regard to colour, and the interaction between white and black populations within a unified nation-state where the white is in a dominant 'host' position and the black is in a subordinate one as colonial migrant. The main emphasis is on racial stigmatisation and its effects on 'race relations'. Social policy recommendations are often made. There are various tendencies within this tradition, ranging from empirical studies of black groups, their economic and housing deprivation in an urban sociology context, to studies of white racism or of the conflict areas within which 'race relations' are played out (Banton, 1977, 1980, Patterson, 1965, Rex and Moore, 1967, Rose and Deakin, 1969, Rex and Tomlinson, 1979, Van den Berghe, 1978, Brown, 1984).

Marxist approaches, on the other hand. contain a number of distinct tendencies, although Miles (1982) has argued that many of the positions share the race relations problematic with Weberians like John Rex (1970, 1973). The most important attempt seeks to understand racism as a constituent of the development of capitalism, and its ongoing effects in modern societies despite its origins being located in slave society or colonial experience (Cox, 1970, Genovese, 1968 and 1974, Sivanandan, 1973). Ethnic and 'race' phenomena tend to be reduced to class phenomena (see the discussion of race and class later in this chapter). Another tendency is the attempt to theorise processes of migration from the point of view of the structural requirements of the mode of production and especially with regard to the role of migrants as categories of labour within developed capitalist nation states (Castles and Kosack, 1973, Castells, 1975, Nikolinakos, 1975, Phizacklea and Miles, 1980). The Marxist approaches share the problem of resolving the question of the distinct effectivity of racial/ethnic categories and locating ethnic and 'race' processes within the constituent elements of the capitalist mode of production.

This chapter provides the theoretical framework for the book. It considers the concepts of ethnic group and ethnicity, discusses the link between ethnic and racial categories, reviews a selection of theoretical positions and finally provides a theoretical framework for addressing these issues.

The Concept of Ethnic Group and the Question of Ethnicity

Ethnicity is a problematic notion and has been subjected to a number of definitions (Weber, 1969, Barth, 1969. Kahn, 1981, Cohen, 1974, Smith, 1987) as well as being found sorely wanting by more radical writers (like Gilroy, 1987). Ethnicity is a term that is often identified with the ethnic studies approach Just as 'race' is identified with the race relations tradition (see Anthias, 1982).

The problem of conceptualising ethnicity is related to the problem of defining an ethnic group as a form of social differentiation. There is also the problem of defining the boundaries of an ethnic group in any concrete case. The definition of an ethnic group is a contested area. Ethnic groups are a modern form of social differentiation, are tied to the development of the nation state and linked to modernity. Religious or linguistic communities are often vital ingredients in the construction of ethnic groups but are not coterminous with them. Ethnic groups are not merely groups that share a distinct culture but formulate themselves according to a common origin and often destiny. They are premised on the development of solidary bonds and consciousness around an imaginary origin (often called a myth of origin) which may be located in diverse ways, historically, culturally or territorially.

The concept of 'ethnic group' has failed to stand as an essential element of a systematic theory of social relations. Within non–Marxist discourse, Weber (1969) and Barth (1969) come closest to giving the concept a clear theoretical status. Weber, in examining ethnic groups seeks for the origins of group structuration:

We shall call ethnic groups those human groups that entertain a subjective belief in their common descent because of similarities of physical type or customs or both (1969:395).

For Weber. ethnic groups are the paradigm case of status organisation and assume significance, like all status groups, in periods of economic stability. Class is regarded as a primary factor in times of economic crisis. However, ethnic communities are particularly important for Weber as they could evolve into full nation states. Ethnic honour had the potential of undercutting economic divisions and unlike other status group manifestations was not dependent on a hierarchical division of economic life chances and their symbolic representation. A central difficulty is that Weber fails to attend to ethnic and class stratification as interlocking and mutually reinforcing aspects of modern society. Nor does he consider the extent to which ethnicity can construct intra-class divisions. Class relations cannot be analysed on the assumption of ethnic homogeneity and where there is a coincidence of class position and ethnic category this provides a greater potential for political mobilisation. Weber saw ethnic identity as being superseded by the rationalisation of social life, epitomised of course by his category of economic action.

Barth (1969), on the other hand, treats ethnic groups as organisational vessels. Ethnicity is regarded as a cognitive category that classifies a person in terms of his most basic, most general identity, presumptively determined by his origin and background (Barth, 1969: 130). Other writers have focused on the question of ethnic identity (eg Shibutani and Kwan, 1969) and the most dominant approaches have treated ethnicity generally as being characterised either by a shared culture or/and a common identity (eg Smith, 1986). This can say nothing about the processes that are involved in the construction and form that attributions of common identity take, however.

Within Marxism, the ethnic category is not a necessary constituent of the abstract mode of production which is blind to the cultural, ethnic or gender attributions of the individuals who fill the 'spaces' (Poulantzas, 1973). That is why difference on ethnic or 'race' grounds is treated as a complicating conjunctural factor, like sexual difference and division, which can be subsumed and often reduced to class relations.

However, if we shift to a different level of analysis, that of the determinate society, both class and ethnic divisions acquire significance as principles of real and ideological differentiations and as a basis for political mobilisation. Both class and ethnic group involve organisation, consciousness and political action. The problem however lies in the material location of their basis. In Marxist discourse the basis for class is given through the hierarchical incorporation of the concept within that of 'mode of production'. The basis for the ethnic category is missing. Therefore, Marxist writers have often sought its basis in some variant of the class form (Anthias, 1990).

Within Marxist discourse therefore, the dominant tendency has been to reduce ethnic and race phenomena to class phenomena. Ethnic groups are seen as incipient classes or possessing false consciousness. Ethnicity as a medium for expressing class interests is found particularly in the work of Africanists (Saul, 1979, Kahn, 1981). Ethnic and racial ideologies are seen as functionally related to capital and many of these analyses evade or sidestep the precise mechanism by which economic processes produce racial or ethnic effects. Later in this chapter the Marxist approach to questions of racism in particular will be considered. Before considering a number of positions in the literature on ethnicity and 'race', I want to look at the connection between ethnic and race phenomena.

Race and Ethnic Categories

Some literature treats 'race' and ethnic groups under one umbrella whereas some literature distinguishes them. There are basically two views on the relationship between ethnic and race categories. One point of view argues that there is nothing distinctive about 'race', so there is no important difference between racial identification and ethnicity. This point of view treats 'race' as a phenomenon within the broader category of ethnic relations – that is as a mere sign of a cultural difference or a 'boundary' marker (Wallman, 1978) – a more pronounced and visible boundary marker but no different in form than others. The other point of view is that 'race' is a distinct phenomenon which is either linked to psychological factors relating to colour or to racial categorisation having a different causality with regard to colonialism and capitalism. From this point of view race relations become the study of racial representations and their economic and social effects. Ethnic relations are then defined as relations between cultures. This is the kind of schema that John Rex (1973) is working with. There is also an ongoing debate about the analytical validity of the notion of 'race' influenced by the work of Guillaumin (1988), presented most succinctly in Miles (1982: 42) view that 'race' is merely a category of every day life and should not be deployed analytically.

One specific view of the distinction between race and ethnic groups is that ethnicity involves allegiance to ancestral descent and is voluntarily maintained whereas race identification is enforced by the majority and those subjected to the definition may be ashamed of their racial identity (Lyon, 1972). From this point of view, it is the individual's subjective experience and orientation that is a defining characteristic. Ethnicity is maintained by volitional internal processes (cultural identity) whereas race is maintained through the imposition of racial or cultural distinctiveness. Although it is true that racial stigmatisation is externally constructed this is not the only form that race identity takes. Race is a social construct that uses cultural, symbolic or phenotypes as markers of a fixed and unchangeable essence. These can have either a positive or negative valuation (after all whites have been defined as a race), can be constructed through the mythology of the group or a mythology or ideology external to the group. They need not be imposed. Indeed racial stigmatisation can lend itself to any difference that can be imputed to an ethnic origin – witness the shifting categories with regard to the Asian and Muslim categories in

Britain and the shifting definitions of 'Black' (Anthias and Yuval Davis, 1992). In addition, so called racially defined groups such as African Caribbeans and Asians possess, like other ethnicities, their own distinct cultures and organisations which develop dynamically in interplay with their social positioning and experience.

In Wallman's (1978) analysis race is a sub category of the ethnic group and involves the construction of certain messages. Colour is a boundary marker for race and denotes readily the dimensions of political and economic structure. But the reasons why a colour boundary should mark an economic boundary need to be explored. For colour itself is not an empirically given dimension of social structure – while Turks in London are 'white' they are 'black' in Germany. Some Cypriots are darker than some Asians and yet they may be regarded and regard themselves as a white or European group. The category of European white is becoming an increasingly used one in differentiating inclusion and exclusion of those who may be legitimately seen to belong to Western European nation states. Colour itself is a social construct and can only function as a visible boundary when it has assumed symbolic significance.

I shall now look at a number of attempts to theorise ethnicity and then look at the race relations problematic of John Rex and a number of Marxist attempts to explore the links with class.

Ethnicity

A major tendency in sociology is to treat ethnicity as merely a question of cultural identity. The influential debate around assimilation (Glazer and Moynihan, 1965) treats ethnicity as a voluntaristic normative identification process or as a form of culture. The notion of 'resurgent' ethnicity reaffirms the view of ethnicity as 'ethnic identity'. Glazer and Moynihan (1975) see ethnic identity as an alternative to national identity whilst class identity is seen as declining. On the other hand Gans (1979) notes the growth of symbolic ethnicity, as a personal affirmation of belonging in American society.

The English ethnic school utilised an approach that treats ethnic groups as mainly cultural communities facing problems of integration and assimilation. Much of the work attempted to provide insights into the culture of ethnic minorities and its meaning for the actors. Jeffery (1976) is interested in processes by which a group maintains its culture, for example. Often a view is expressed (eg in Dahya, 1974 and Wallman, 1979) that ethnic groups as distinct cultures will choose certain occupations or forms of social participation.

In her review of the sociology of race relations in Britain, Bourne (1980) argues against this approach in terms of its necessary political effects. But no theorisation has necessary political effects nor can it be countered by saying that its empirical premises are mistaken. The central difficulty with the ethnic school approach is the way it formulated ethnicity either as identity or shared culture, and the role it assigned to these in

14

understanding the placement of ethnic groups in society. Wallman for example states that

> the effect of (their) ethnicity is therefore dependent on the state of the economic system and on their bargaining position within it. Conversely they will not see, will not accept, will not succeed in the opportunity offered if it is not appropriate to their choice of work or their cultural experience (1979: 14).

Ethnicity has become defined as a static cultural property that informs actors choices, rather than as a dynamic relation to particular socio economic and political structures.

The notion of reactive ethnicity, advanced by the school, saw it as a cultural affirmation, resulting from the individual sense of rejection that members of ethnic groups (in the Ballards' case Asians (1977)) face. This is grounded in a passive and personally instrumental response. Hechter (1975), from a rational choice position, also puts forward a reactive theory of ethnicity and argues that it does not necessarily arise out of cultural differentiation. Reactive theory argues that ethnic solidarity develops when individuals are assigned to specific types of occupation on the basis of observable cultural traits. Ethnicity is directed against the basis of exploitation and domination in a specific form of social system characterised by cores and peripheries. A major problem with the model Hechter develops is that it is the ethnicity of the dominant group that leads to the reactive ethnicity of the dominated, and thus he assumes that which he tries to explain.

The focus on relations between cultures and identities is one of the reasons why Gilroy (1987) rejects the concept of ethnicity. However, Stuart Hall (1988) has attempted to retrieve the term from the conceptual baggage of the ethnic approach by his location of ethnicity as a subjective identification process that forms part of the fragmentation of post-modern society. For Hall (1989) ethnic and cultural difference are synonymous. They relate to origins, roots, traditions, identities and although relational, they construct belonging rather than exclusion.

For Hall, ethnicity need not be essentialist for it may be premised on a commonality of experience rather than origin as in the case of 'Black' being treated as a community through the common experience of racism, despite distinct histories and traditions. Ethnicity may be a mode for rejecting 'Other' attributions and a product of a politics of culture and identity emphasising common experience rather than ancestry. However, this form of ethnicity is often dedicated to discovering a unifying point of origin as in the case of black nationalism (the back to Africa movement). A Black identity has foundered indeed on the failure to ground an ethnic commonality in a distinct origin (and it may be argued also on a different experience of racism) for African-Caribbeans and Asians in particular (Anthias and Yuval Davis 1992). On the other hand, the development of Asian identity is very much a political development in the context of migration and a racist society that unites together distinct regional, linguistic and religious groups such as those from India and Pakistan, or

Moslems and Sikhs. A fairly recent development is the centrality of religious identity for constructing community as in the case of the Muslim category in the aftermath of the Rushdie affair.

Hall makes a sharp distinction between ethnicity and 'race'. The former is seen to provide the individual with a sense of belonging and with roots and is not essentialist, whereas race constructs the Other as fixed, natural and hailed by the self– evident attribute of not being the same. For Hall 'race' serves to deny the validity of others whereas ethnicity recognises that we are all positioned in a historical and cultural context and recognises the validity of others.

This is in great contrast to the earlier location of ethnicity within the discourse of culturalist and subjectivist forms of social theory (eg the ethnic school approach) and presents an interesting distinction.

John Rex and the Race Relations Problematic

Rex's work provides a bridge between the ethnic studies and a Marxist approach that sees ethnic and race categories as essentially economic and class categories. John Rex is a Weberian, concerned with class as it relates to the differential access to resources (at the level of distribution) rather than production. His work on race is specifically concerned with the position of black groups but he posits a general theory related to colonialism and class exclusion that is clearly also applicable to non–black ethnic groups in a migrant context. For Rex, the 'under–class' nature of colonial immigrants (note than he does not use the term migrant labour) consists in their inferior position within the working class and in the fact that they are politically separate from the organised labour movement. However, factors which structure the position of colonial immigrants within the market and politically (he conceptualises ethnic (Black) politics in terms of defensive confrontation) are never clearly specified and conflate the economic requirements of capital with discrimination practices by human actors.

Rex has contributed both to the debate on the links between colonialism and race and the links between race and class and can be seen, despite his Weberianism, in terms of a tradition established by the black Marxist writer Oliver Cox (1970). This is a mode of argument that reduces races to false ideological categories constituted through the medium of class relations– racism becomes a medium for the rationalisation and reinforcement of exploitation required by the economic system. A problem that is common to this tradition is that false racial stereotypes are left to the construction of individual consciousness (of capitalists for Cox and workers for Rex), in the absence of a mechanism by which the mode of production actually produces ideological effects. An additional problem is that any postulate of the origins of racism does not in itself adequately explain the structural conditions which account for its contemporary effectivity.

According to Rex 'race relations' are a category of class relations and not ethnic relations. Whilst Rex seems to be reducing race to class, he also seems to be working with some notion of what ethnic relations might be that remains unspecified. Also if 'race relations' are a category of class relations and race is about Black versus White groups, then he is positing the existence of two classes, one White and one Black. Class relations then come to signify relations between these two groups rather than relations between a capitalist class and a proletariat.

A central difficulty for Rex is to account on the one hand for his depiction of 'race relations as a category of class relations' and on the other hand for race relations problems as:

> relating to the transfer of individuals and groups, whose structured position has previously been defined in colonial terms of some kind, to positions as workers or traders into metropolitan society itself (Rex, 1981: 17).

Whereas the first depiction reduces race to class, the second focuses on the colonial origin of workers rather than their economic role. It is the valuation then of individuals with a colonial heritage that structures their underclass position rather than their actual placement. The colonial heritage is responsible for the stigmatisation of black workers by the white working class who consider them then as outsiders or competitors. Rex is positing a political division between 'natives' and 'outsiders' within the working class. A further problem here is that he assumes a homogeneous indigenous class, not already divided.

Finally, although for Rex, class and ethnic organisation become alternative bases for immigrant organisation, he is unclear as to what provides the form of consciousness of ethnic organisation and action, particularly in relation to the extent to which it is a particular form of class action or what its class effects are.

I have argued that Rex's depiction of race relations as class relations and the ways in which he privileges the colonial context in structuring racial stigmatisation presents some theoretical difficulties. I have also argued that the stress on the stigmatisation of groups through the prior seizing of state power by 'natives' assumes a homogeneous White working class and also a Black/White divide. The final result is to reduce both race and class to the idealist representations of social actors. The structural location of migrants becomes reduced to the expression and effects of a racial ideology that has become a psycho-social mechanism for the pursuit of principles of economic rational interests by actors.

I shall now turn to considering three Marxist informed approaches that attempt to explore the link between 'race' and class phenomena.

Theorisations of Race and Class

The identification of race as some form of class relation is a well-charted as well as disputed position that has dominated most of the literature and debate that is tied to Marxism, as well as forming a particular strand in much mainstream analysis of race and ethnicity, particularly in its Weberian variant (despite the distinct conceptual categories that are employed). Miles has suggested in fact that 'the race relations problematic' is shared by Weberians (like Rex) and Marxists (like Sivanandan, 1976, 1983, 1986) and the authors of the Empire Strikes Back (CCCS, 1982),

> because they attribute the ideological notion of race with descriptive and explanatory importance (Miles, 1984: 218).

Oliver Cox (1970) is often credited as the major fore-runner to the contemporary formulation of 'race and class' but as Miles (1980) and Gabriel and Ben-Tovim (1978) have shown, in different ways, there is as much connection with Weber as with Marx. Cox equated race with colour. He saw a distinction between discrimination on the basis of ethnicity and of race (colour). Discrimination on the basis of race was regarded as developing out of class interests, ie as a mode for justifying economic exploitation. For Cox, racism grew out of capitalism and provided a means for furthering the use of labour as a commodity, resulting in a greater exploitation which was legitimated through ideas of racial difference and inferiority. It was the use to which physical difference (ie colour) was put in the interests of capital which constituted racism.

Castles and Kosack (1973) epitomise an approach that superimposes economic categories on migrant categories:

> We may therefore speak of two strata within the working class: the indigenous workers with generally better conditions and the feeling of no longer being at the bottom of society, form the higher stratum. The immigrants, who are the most underprivileged and exploited group of society, form the lower stratum (: 477).

It's worth pointing out that in Castles' more recent work the emphasis has shifted to a less economistic and functionalist analysis (Castles, 1986). Indeed this is characteristic of more contemporary debates within Marxism which have been around the issue of developing a non-reductionist analysis of the links between race and class as well as in the understanding of other non-class social relations such as gender.

There are a number of ways in which approaches to the relations between race and class may be categorised (Miles, 1982, Solomos, 1986 and Gilroy, 1987). I have chosen to make the following distinctions:
1. Approaches that see 'racial' groups as an underclass, as a subordinate stratum within the working class or separated from the white working class.
2. Approaches that are concerned with the role of migrant labour within the capitalist mode of production. These often see migrants as a class fraction within the working class or as a reserve army of labour for capital.
3. Approaches that focus on racist ideology seeing it as the product either in a strong or a weak way of class interests and historically linked to colonialist economic relations. Alternatively racism is seen as strictly ideological and as having a relative autonomy from class or as fully autonomous.

4. Approaches that see 'race' as producing its own conditions of struggle which are important for class structuration or formation ie it is the articulation of race and class that is important.

Writers may use more than one of these formulations. For example, the work of Castles and Kosack (1973) mentioned earlier and of Phizacklea and Miles (1980) span a number of these foci. I shall now discuss briefly approaches 2, 3 and 4. The first approach has been discussed already with reference to the work of Rex.

Migrant Labour as a Class Fraction

Phizacklea and Miles (1980) central argument is that black migrants are a class fraction of the working class. The colonialist heritage of migrant labour structures their specific position as a class fraction and allows them a specific political/legal role in the capitalist social formation. This in addition allows them to be used as cheap labour. Phizacklea and Miles explicitly focus on the category of migrant labour rather than racial group, and particularly on colonial migrant labour which for them means racialised or Black migrant labour :

> the colonisation process has had as one of its features the direct politico–ideological domination of the colonised social formation such that there was direct or indirect political rule and the development of an ideology alleging the inferiority of the dominated (1980: 10).

Migrant labour theory differs from many Marxist approaches to race in as much as the problematic focusses on migration as providing a supply of labour power through a process of geographical and economic displacement which becomes inserted into the capitalist mode. It is not specifically concerned with the question of racist ideology and its effects. However, depicting black migrant labour as a class fraction does not specify the articulation of the racial with migrant labour (as opposed to migrant labour without racialisation). It also underemphasises the heterogeneity of labour categories it presents and the distinct employment characteristics of Asians, African–Caribbeans and other colonial migrants (such as Cypriots) is not raised. To what extent does this heterogeneity problematise the unitary application of 'class fraction'? Finally, and most importantly, the migrant labour problematic fails to consider the 40 per cent of Britain's black population who are not 'migrant' and the concern to show the class bases of black migrant labour serves to underplay divisions within the black population. There is in fact a conflation in the problematic and categories used since migrant labour is the focus but this Is equated with racialised groups.

Despite some of the difficulties with this approach the problematic of migrant labour Is a useful one. Even though the British experience has been one of a settler population from a colonial region, restrictions on migration and on citizenship have occurred In relation to this population, that make treating them (or at least sections) as having a distinct political–ideological position increasingly pertinent.

Castells (1975) has also argued that the political legal status of migrant labour in Europe constitutes it as a class fraction but he is not concerned with racialisation. For Castells it is precisely the legal and political conditions of migrant labour that are important. The terms of contract and entry constitute them as a necessary, but particular, input to capitalism at the centre. It also prevents their incorporation into the class structure on any other terms which has pertinent effects in fragmenting the working class.

In relation to Britain, we would have to show a distinct political legal position to the migrant worker category as such, and not that a section (for colonial or economic reasons) have become racialised. In Britain, migrants have different political/ideological positions linked to country of origin, year of entry, extent of racial discrimination, employment and so on. Their political–ideological position cannot be extrapolated merely from their 'migrant status'. Phizacklea and Miles however argue that de facto discrimination can be theoretically equivalent to de jure discrimination. But this latter occurs not only in relation to migrants who are Black but the British born Black population (as well as migrants from Southern Europe and other third world migrant workers).

The real social ensemble referred to by Phizacklea and Miles is in fact not migrant labour but the Black population. To argue that the whole of this population then constitutes a class fraction would necessitate that they had a particular class position, and can be identified in class terms. Although it is true that Black people have a tendency to be clustered within the manual class categories, there is great variation both between different ethnic minorities and within them. To further argue that they are a distinct fraction (as opposed to stratum which merely requires that they be identified in the lower reaches) requires that they have a distinct political organisational position. But the ways in which Afro–Caribbeans and Asians are organising during this latest phase of the race relations industry (Modood, 1989), has become increasingly differentiated which makes this depiction problematic.

In fact, when we attend closely to the argument, it is clear that in the final analysis, for Phizacklea and Miles, it is racist ideology (because of the central role accorded to de facto discrimination in constituting black people as a class fraction), rather than say the requirements of capital or the economic categories of migrant labour, that structure the economic position of black people and the political legal relations they are inserted into. Class position, then, becomes an effect of colour and its signifying role within racist discourse.

Race as Ideological

Gabriel and Ben Tovim (1980 and 1981) (a more extended account of this position is given in Solomos, 1986) share the view with both Rex and Miles and Phizacklea that race is ideological, but for them it is an

20

autonomous ideological category that then becomes inserted into economic relations:

> If we are to achieve a satisfactory resolution to the concepts of race and racism, then clearly they must be seen as concepts whose objects are ideological .... the product ..... of determinate ideological practices, with their own theoretical/ideological conditions of existence and their own irreducible contradictions. Only subsequent to this process of ideological production do specific racial ideologies intervene at the level of political practice and the economy (1978: 139).

For this view, racism is to be combated by democratic populist ideology rather than economic changes and it becomes essentially a policy rather than a class issue. What has occurred in this formulation is an opposite effect to the earlier ones where race had been defined as a product essentially of class which is the privileged domain of effectivity within capitalIst social relations. Here, following a broadly Althusserian (1970) conception of social relations, we have race merely present in ideology and thus fractured from class or other forms of social relation which are then seen as non-ideological. This reification of race as inalienable and unsubjected to determinations other than those of ideology appears as an almost inevitable outcome of remaining within the terms of the earlier debates but disagreeing with the epistemological primacy given to class or economic relations.

Taking on board some of these difficulties with conceptualising race as linked to class, Miles's more recent work considers race as ideological and rejects the concept of race:

> I do not believe it is defensible or worthwhile to construct or pursue a sociology or race relations.....The task is not to analyse 'race relations' but to explain, inter alia, why the category of 'race relations' came to be used to categorise a certain group of social relations which, once examined from a different perspective, cannot be shown to be essentially distinct from other social relations (Miles, 1982).

Miles position presents a highly attractive challenge to the race relations problematic. Racism is regarded as an ideology and Miles distinguishes between processes of generation and reproduction of ideologies (and their transformation) and therefore, like Gabriel and Ben Tovim it is a question of developing a specific analysis of ideologies in particular historical contexts.

Race and Class Formation

Paul Gilroy (1987), like Miles, offers a challenging reformulation of the links between race and class and he falls into the final typology mentioned earlier. The position he takes can essentially be seen as a development of Stuart Hall's view (1980) that race is as important in class formation and

21

structuration as class is in race structuration. Using the concept of articulation, Hall remains within the framework of the debate in seeing race and class as separate but connected sets of relations but with a form of agnosticism (relative autonomy) concerning which is primary. Hall's famous and powerful phrase that 'race is the modality in which class is lived' (Hall et al, 1978: 394) also assumes that class consciousness, presumably unlike race consciousness, is never at the point of being but always in the process of becoming. Class therefore requires something else (ie race) as its representational or phenomenal form.

Gilroy too rejects the view that race and class are reducible to each other or that racist ideology is a product of class relations or merely has ongoing effects on class relations. Rather, he argues that race is an essential ingredient in the history of class formation and structuration in British society:

> The class character of black struggles is not a result of the fact that blacks are predominantly proletarian, though this is true. It is established in the fact that their struggles for civil rights, freedom from state harassment, or as waged workers are instances of the process by which the working class is constituted politically, organised in politics (Gilroy, 1982: 302).

For Gilroy, race must problematise our thinking around class. He is antagonistic to the notion of ethnicity although he insists that black communities are not only organised through their common experience of racism but are also cultural communities. Gilroy wants to introduce a

> more sophisticated theory of culture into the political analysis of race and racism by claiming the term back from ethnicity (198: 17).

He is clearly arguing with the way this term has often been used in an essentialist way. For Gilroy 'racial meanings are not part of ideology but part of culture'. Although he fails to clarify the ways in which he is differentiating these terms it is clear that his rejection of the idea of race as ideological is an assertion of the reality of racially organised communities and that any analysis must take this reality seriously. Gilroy argues that class and other differentiations such as sex and race have 'different histories of subordination' and as pointed out earlier 'cannot be empirically disentangled'. For Gilroy, the antagonisms around race are not limited to those concerned with production. Race is a process which is historically constructed and he is concerned with the:

> manner in which racial meanings, solidarity and identities provide the basis for action.

These are both an:

> Alternative to class consciousness at the political level and a factor in the very formation of classes (1987: 27).

Essentially he is suggesting that both class and race involve forms of social subordination that inform each other at the level of consciousness,

22

organisation and meaning, but he has not been able to posit the axis for race. This is largely because he fails to treat race in terms of ideas and practices relating to ethnic and national collectivities and how they are understood and used under particular social, political and economic conditions.

Central Problems

There are a number of central problems that are shared by most of these positions. Firstly, theoretical shifts will often occur concerning the object of analysis. For example where the object is migrant labour, a shift may occur to migrant groups, ethnic or racial groups or Black (often meaning Afro Caribbean) groups. A conflation takes place between migrant labour as a particular category of labour and certain ascriptive characteristics defining group formation (eg black, ethnic). Where a racial or ethnic group is identified as a class, class stratum or class fraction, this assumes that it is homogeneously constituted in relation to production, that classes themselves are ethnically homogeneous and ignores intra class and intra ethnic divisions. Where migrant groups, racial groups or migrant labour are defined as a reserve army of labour, conceptual and empirical problems occur in relation to the use of Marxist economic categories to an inappropriate object (Anthias, 1981).

A second problem is that there often occurs a conflation between different levels of abstraction which leads to the conflation of different kinds of questions. At one level we can try to conceptualise the role of racial or ethnic categories within the capitalist mode of production but since such a mode does not require ethnic differences we must resort to explaining their role within the concrete mode of production that always exists within a determinate social formation. Here a tendency has been to see race as reducible to the ideological representation of class–as a kind of false consciousness.

A third difficulty lies in the failure to specify the precise effects of racial categorisation on labour categories. If it is racism that determines the incorporation (and exclusions) at the economic level then economic requirements must be seen as secondary. What generally happens is the racism is seen as constituted in colonialist social relations and then is seen to have its effects in the present.

Finally, there is the question of the heterogeneity of the class and economic categories found within what can be regarded as a racialised population In Britain even if we only use the signifier of colour (this ignores the other victims of systemic racism, such as so called White Commonwealth migrants, like Cypriots and third world migrant workers). There is no space here to look at this issue empirically but there are a number of publications that provide data on the labour categories of different groups (Gordon and Newnham, 1986, Newnham, 1986). The growth of self–employment amongst Asians, particularly as a response to unemployment, and the high unemployment levels of young Blacks and of Black women are central differentiating factors.

23

A particular issue is whether, even where we cannot refer to race as some variant of class relations struggles around racism or ethnicity construct a unity (a commonality of interests, consciousness and action) that cuts across the class, gender or cultural divisions within racialised groups. Certainly ethnic commonality can function in the interests of capital, as in the use of ethnic labour, or the formation of an English national unity (Anthias, 1983 and Anthias and Yuval Davis, 1992). But can the opposite work, uniting worker and small capitalist in class action forged through common experience and struggle around culture, ethnicity or racism? Gilroy's (1987) view is that the experience of the structures and culture of racism is only one of the factors in racial solidarity and that black people in Britain have a distinct mode of culture and organisation. The extent to which race or class solidarity wins the day, however, is a question of political priorities in specific contexts. They cannot, however, be disaggregated easily as race structuration takes place In the context of class, is one of its conditions of existence and class structuration in Britain has been within the context of race.

In relation to racism, it has become increasingly inadequate to locate it as the product of class interests at the level of production, both because racism is not a necessary prerequisite of class exploitation (although it may, like gender, facilitate it) and also because class is increasingly no longer understood only with reference to the relations of production but also with reference to struggles located elsewhere. Also racism crosscuts class, as for example in racism towards middle class Blacks and other minority groups. Racism however can be used for class purposes and often representational, political and institutional processes relating to 'racial' differences are developed with particular reference to class political interests. Racism can be used to further the interests of specific classes within dominant and aspiring dominant ethnic groups, where ethnic supremacy will involve the privileged exploitation or access to economic or polItIcal resources. Similarly race discourse can be used to articulate struggle around economic and political power and resources, as a medium of class action. However, given the heterogeneity of economic position withIn and between racialised groups, racism, as some unitary phenomenon working on a supposed homogeneous category of 'race' producing class effects cannot be maintained.

Towards a Theoretical Framework for Theorising Ethnicity and Racism – the Construct of Ethnos

A major problem in conceptualising ethnic and 'race' phenomena is that their understanding requires incorporating them into an analysis of the ways in which difference and identity are constructed as pegs for inferiorisation, subordination and exploitation, ie as relations of economic and political exclusions and inequalities. The concrete relations that are defined as ethnic or racial are not explicable as products of ethnic or race processes but require consideration of wider social relations including those of gender and class. Often there is a conflation between the analytical separation of the categories of ethnic, class and gender divisions and their consideration as distinct sets of concrete social relations which are then seen to interconnect in some essential way (Anthias, 1990). Rather, in concrete social relations they are intermeshed in specific and very diverse ways. The theoretical outcomes of the position I have taken involve a number of propositions:

(a) That there are no 'real' or essential ethnic groups, races or nations as opposed to false ones. Ethnic, racial and national groups are all attributed and proclaimed, from the outside and from the inside, using various claims to difference and identity such as history, culture, biology, territory etc (this does not however make them merely ideological in as much as the attributions and proclamations are embedded in concrete practices and relations). These claims are dynamic and shift over time. For example, ethnic groups can come to redefine themselves or be redefined as national, racial or religious groups.

b) The transformation of the claims is linked to political projects and may be the outcome of state and other discourses in interplay with the economic and cultural resources or aims of the groups themselves or others. This means that there are no necessary ways in which ethnic and race processes present themselves within wider social relations. Race and ethnic categories have to be understood with reference to political, economic and cultural processes (since they involve placement along the dimensions of power involved in all the ways by which collective subjects are identified) and cannot be understood with reference to any generic ethnic or race process (for example to do with merely the interaction between ethnic groups as minority majority relations or any other way this has been formulated.)

c) Race and ethnic categories have to be understood within a framework which also recognises the ways in which gender and class categories (which the same individuals are divided into) function to place, exclude and inferiorise and some of the contradictions and overdeterminations this results in. This presents particular problems for anti-racism, anti-sexism and equal opportunities programmes. A cultural practice that is fostered as anti-racist may be sexist and vice versa.

The contested nature of the concepts of racism, ethnicity and nationalism is clear as are those of gender, sexual difference and class. They all refer however, to modes by which difference and identity become attributed and proclaimed. Identity (with) and difference (from) are treated here as pertaining to the available modes. rules, social practices and societal and state processes which construct and facilitate identification. To identify with is to differentiate from and vice versa. In this sense difference and identity are relational and logically require each other.

The attributions and identifications are not static or given nor on the other hand are they totally arbitrary. They are part of a social ontology which posits a taxonomy that is dichotomous eg insider and outsider, black versus white, men versus women, capitalist versus worker. The dichotomies constructed in the case of class will depend on the theoretical and political position taken. Such dichotomous taxonomies are characteristic of Western thought. Such a social ontology also involves a taxonomy of spheres of existential location with regard to sexuality (gender), collectivity and belongingness (ethnic) and economic positioning (class).

The categorial formations thus produced set out places to be filled by collective subjects who possess the appropriate attributes or identifications. In the last instance however they all become represented in biological, primordial or genetic ways which fix them. This is seen most clearly where gender is regarded as the manifestation of sexual difference and in certain types of ethnic categorisation (particularly race) as well as being found in explanations of genetic difference in class position. The biological or essentially based difference is seen as manifested in social outcomes. The social outcomes are however produced via the intervention of modes by which inferiority, subordination and exploitation are incorporated within political practices in their broadest sense and encompass the family, the state and the nation.

The construction of difference and identity in the case of ethnic phenomena involves a positioning with regard to collectivity and belongingness and sets up a boundary of who can and who can't belong to a particular population along lines of some origin or destiny of the group signified by historical. biological, linguistic, cultural, religious or 'stock' attributions. It is not these that characterise ethnic groups but the claims that are made on their basis for a natural community of people. As already mentioned who can and who can't be included may change over time. Relations around sexuality and gender are central in defining the boundaries of the ethnic group and the state will often construct and harness these relations to pursue specific ethnic, national is well as class projects (Anthias and Yuval Davis, 1989). From this point of view, 'race' is one type of attribution of collective difference and identity.

I shall now turn to arguing the links between ethnicity, race, racism and nationalism using the notion of ethnos.

The Construct of Ethnos and Connecting Race and Ethnic Phenomena

The construct of ethnos (cf Smith, 1986) is treated here both as highly differentiated in its historical manifestations and as providing an umbrella construct for conceptualising the phenomena of ethnicity, nationalism and those of racism. The historical manifestations of ethnicity, nationalism and racism are not merely derivative of ethnos however. The form that attributions and political projects of ethnos take will partly depend on the way that class and other economic and political interests come to overdetermine those of ethnos or collectivity. In order to clarify this a differentiation is made between ethnos on the one hand as the umbrella category and ethnicity, nationalism and racism as forms of discourse and practice that constitute different modes for articulating a collective

26

originary claim, which may indeed be informed by nation building or economic projects.

The term 'ethnos' in Greek means nation but the way it is used here is not restricted to the political or territorial imperatives found in nationhood as we understand it in the modern era. Ethnos here is used to denote all those phenomena that involve the following:

(a) An attribution of difference from the Other and identification within of a group of subjects or a population in terms of a supposed common or shared origin. This may be focused around language, tradition, culture, heritage, history, territory or generic 'stock'.

(b) The formation of a self-conscious political project around any of these. This distinguishes a passive or taken for granted sense of belonging or identity from the formation of ethnic groups as such. In order for this consciousness to arise it must be relational to an Other either in the sense of constructing one or being constructed as one.

(c) There is always a political dimension. This may be essentially defensive or offensive, exclusionary or usurpationary (Parkin, 1979). Its character is given by the context in relation to the distribution of resources within a division of labour also structured by class and gender relations.

(d) Ethnos specifies boundaries which involve mechanisms of inclusion and exclusion of individuals and categorise them into those that can and those that cannot belong to a given population and share its attributions and resources. This occurs at a number of different levels; structural/ systemic (eg through the state) and discursive /action (eg through beliefs, prescriptions, ideologies, images or intersubjectivities).

Despite the great heterogeneity of the phenomena of ethnos a commonality exists in two ways: by the construction or representation of a group origin as providing claims to common identity and by an imaginary or imagery of common culture, language, territory and so on that belong as an inalienable right to the group. In this sense ethnos involves the construction of an origin as a significant arena for collective identity and action. This identity may be constructed from outside as well as inside the group. Ethnicity, nationalism, race and racism can be located as belonging to this group of phenomena.

Ethnic processes are always relational. Difference and identity are premised on each other as are inclusion and exclusion. However, the form in which these occur is diverse and need not be antagonistic or hierarchical. This is where identities on the basis of the category of cultural difference have to be distinguished from ethnic identity. The former need not involve a notion of identification on the basis of either origin or claims to an essential culture nor the formation of oppositional or exclusionary boundaries – class, cultural, regional or youth cultures do not hail the kind of essence that characterises ethnic phenomena. The ethnic category is also more all encompassing and the illusion of collective destiny serves to refuse and deny crosscutting divisions within the group (Gellner, 1988).

27

It is not possible to dispense with the concept of race as Miles (1982) has argued nor to see race as independent from the ethnic category as Omi and Winant (1987) have maintained. This is so despite the fact that the bases for racial categorisation are always mythological and invalid and that ethnic processes in general do not constitute an adequate explanation for the form or content of racial attributions, consciousness or racist ideologies and practice.

To reject 'race' must mean also to reject `ethnic' for both refer to claims that are made for positing difference and identity. Both 'race' and `ethnic group' have a similar analytical status, although scientific racial typologies are clearly and unequivocally discredited. However, what race and ethnic categories share is that they are different ways of signifying a given population that is regarded as a natural community of people. Race uses the notion of stock or biological difference which fixes it, whereas ethnic groups may use a number of different notions, like history, culture, territory, language, religion. From this point of view, race is a particular articulation of a boundary relating to a social ontology around collectivity and belongingness. It is important however, to separate the ontological premise of race from processes and discourses of racialisation and racism. Miles (1982) position rejects 'race' but uses the term racialisation which I understand to be different from racism in denoting the process by which a group is identified as a 'race'. But this therefore requires us to treat the construction of 'race' categories seriously, but to abandon the notion of 'race'. But if the notion of `race' is abandoned, it prevents the specification of what has been produced by the process of racialisation.

Having argued for a commonality to ethnic phenomena there are important differences in the discourses and practices of ethnicity, nationalism and racism.

Ethnicity

The question of ethnicity has become increasingly relevant with the rise of ethno-nationalism, regionalism and ethnic secessionism. The current multiculturalist phase of the race relations industry has also played a role in promoting an interest in ethnic identities and cultures in British society. Ethnicity, however, cannot be understood exclusively in terms of a purely voluntaristic, normative identification process as is often assumed, nor is it a unitary phenomenon. Indeed the notion of ethnicity needs to be unpacked and specified for it is used to refer to widely different subjective and structural situations. It is also being increasingly recognised that ethnic processes should not be considered in isolation from other modes of social differentiation such as class and gender (Anthias and Yuval-Davis, 1983). Ethnicity cannot be depicted merely as an effect of ethnic grouping nor as a homologising category without reference to class, political or gender divisions. Ethnicity is constructed using the ethnic group or category as a peg or basis but is not the direct outcome of a cultural, linguistic or other difference upon which an ethnic collective may premise it's construction of a shared origin or culture. Ethnicity is the active face of ethnic consciousness and action and it's expression may take diverse forms and be informed by political projects that are linked to class or other processes.

Ethnicity is neither merely an effect of ethnic grouping nor is it a homologising category. Ethnicity at its most general level involves being socially located within a particular group and sharing its conditions of existence. This will include not only being regarded as having the right credentials for membership from the 'inside' but also being able to muster ethnic resources which can be used for struggle, negotiation and the pursuit of political projects both at the level of the individual but also for the group as a whole in relation to other groups (see Hechter, 1987). Ethnic resources can be economic, territorial, cultural and linguistic amongst others (Anthias, 1982).

Ethnicity is more than merely a question of ethnic identity either in the personal sense vis a vis the individuals identification with a group (as the term is used in the British Ethnic school) or in terms of a shared culture of symbols and meanings that lead to a collective sense of identity or a common experience. Ethnicity involves partaking of the social conditions of a group which is positioned in a particular way in terms of the social allocation of resources, within a context of difference to other groups as well as commonalities and differences within (in relation to the divisions of class and gender for example within the group). Ethnicity cross-cuts gender and class divisions but at the same time involves the positing of a similarity (on the inside) and a difference (from the outside) that seeks to transcend these divisions.

Indeed the existence of a conscious ethnic identity may not even be a necessary condition for the existence of ethnicity. Ethnicity may be constructed outside the group by the material conditions it faces and by its social representation by other groups or by the state. For example migrant labourers from different ethnic origins may become ethnicised through state legislation and by the ways they are identified by the indigenous population; this is the sort of ethnicity that Hall partly refers to when he refers to the role of common experience as distinct from a common origin. However, in practice ethnic identity and often solidarity will occur either as a pre-requisite for the group or as a result of its material, political or Ideological placement.

The conditions of reproduction of ethnic groups as well as their transformation are centrally linked to the other prime social divisions of class and gender. For example class homogeneity within the group will produce a greater cohesion of interests and goals. Access to the State Apparatus will often lead to the cultural hegemony of one group over others and a subsequent naturalisation of its specific cultural symbols and practices leading to the imposition of its world view in society at large. Women are central in ethnic/ national reproduction and transformation not only as biological reproducers of the members of the group or central in the transmission of its cultural artifacts but also as markers of the boundaries of collectivities (Anthias and Yuval Davis, 1989).

Ethnicity can be conceptualised as a basis for the pursuit of political projects which at times may militate against those of class. One of the powers of the ethnic discourse is that it can draw on 'more proximate and recognisable ingredients than other ideologies' (Saul, 1979). Indeed, ethnicity can draw upon ideologies of naturalism, as does sexism, ideologies that have a pervasive role both as systematic discourses but also as the constituting element of ideology itself (Althusser, 1971).

However, it is the contention here that no essence can be found to the form in which the political dimension is integral to ethnic processes. Ethnic groups may formulate and be formulated (from the outside as well as the inside) in the furtherance of diverse political projects which includes those of class and nation building (Anthias, 1990).

It is clear then that from this position ethnicity cannot be treated as a static cultural baggage or merely as a process of identification. Nor can it be treated as a unitary phenomenon for it may be centrally organised around culture or around experience or around history as either origin or indeed destiny. In addition the outcomes of ethnic cultural practices have to be considered in terms of the class and gender divisions that are always found within ethnic cultures.

Race and Racisms

Race is a particular articulation of where and how the boundary is constructed between those who can and those who cannot belong to a given population or group. The boundary is formulated around an attributed essence of difference which divides populations in terms of stock or the collective heredity of traits. This is often based on a physiognomic or phenotypical difference or alternatively a cultural difference which is regarded as an expression of an immutable or fixed essence. However, the explication of racisms cannot be undertaken by looking at either ethnic or race phenomena but has to be understood with reference to wider social relations that include those of class, gender and the state. In addition groups regarded as ethnic may become racialised under particular political and economic conditions so that there is no group that concretely can be placed in one or other category. It is the way groups are represented that is important.

Race, therefore, denotes a particular way in which difference comes to be constructed and therefore understood. It cannot be reduced to class (Anthias, 1990) nor can it be erased from the analytical map as Miles (1982) for example suggests.

Racism is linked to 'race' when this supposed difference is used for making claims to the exclusion from full participation in economic, political and social life of the groups of subjects thus defined. However claims for exclusion, subordination and inferiorisation can occur on the basis of ethnic difference more generally as well as, of course, on the basis of class, gender, age and so on. Racist discourse in fact is characterised by the use of ethnic categorisations (which might be constructed around cultural, linguistic or territorial boundaries, as well as supposed biological ones) as signifiers of a fixed, immutable and deterministic difference which acts as a basis for exclusion, subordination and at times of exploitation and oppression. Racist discourse has as a central component the positing of as Cohen puts it 'genealogies of generic difference' (Cohen, 1988: 19).

It is clear that such a definition of racism recognises the existence of different racisms and that it is not a uniformly constituted phenomenon. Different arguments representations and practices can be used for articulating the exclusion / subordination/ exploitation project–as Stuart Hall (1980) notes race may indeed be the modality in which class lives. Racist discourse can focus on different ingredients ranging from arguments relating to superior claims to a legitimate control over national territory (eg Margaret Thatcher's fear of being swamped) to scientific racism found in arguments about the genetic intelligence or capacities of groups, to cultural stereotyping and claims to superior culture. Racism in this sense uses various means for the setting up and legitimation of exclusions that essentially meet projects that at different times are informed by nationalist, class or other struggles for dominance. In other words although the axis for race is to be found in that of ethnos this is not the case for racisms. These are heterogeneously and contextually constituted–in material relations and struggles around them.

Although there are different types of racism what they share is the assertion of an essence to a given population that can then be used for exclusion or subordination purposes. However, there is also a form of racism that is immanent in a series of effects that are not a consequence of either an intentionality by actors or able to be read off from a discourse of inferiorisation or difference and identity. Whereas racism as a set of attributions is embodied in daily language, texts, practices (eg law and education) and in fact the dominant Weltanschauung of a period, racism as a set of outcomes does not require a discourse of difference but merely a set of procedures which categorise people in terms of logistic or juridical criteria. It is here where groups that may not ostensibly face racialisation in discourse may become racialised by the effects of structures (for example where categories of so–called 'white' minorities my be subjected to the racist effects of housing and education policy) without experiencing direct racial discrimination or intersubjective forms of racism, both of which result from discursive racism.

A further dimension to racism however that needs to be incorporated does involve the intersubjective sphere, that is that racism functions at the day to day level as a product of the interrelationships in concrete contexts (that are not themselves intersubjectively constituted) of ethnicised and racialised human subjects within a relation of dominance, economically, politically and culturally. In this sense, the whole dimension of racial and ethnic consciousness and identity are crucial elements in the analysis particularly of resistance to racism but also the modes by which it Is perpetuated or transformed.

Conclusion

Ethnic group and ethnicity are not coterminous. Ethnicity is not merely subjective identification, shared culture or being accepted by an ethnic group. Ethnicity involves an active setting up of boundaries, exclusionary or usurpationary, and is the active face of cultural identity. However, ethnicity and racism can mobilise groups across the boundaries of class and can function to obfuscate class divisions or may be their catalyst. Ethnicity, however, cannot be reduced to class. It's material basis is found in the development of distinct linguistic, cultural and political communalities. The difference that is constructed may provide the basis for divisions, conflicts and for struggle. The 'essence' that is often invoked has broader ideological implications, through ideology's role in postulating the relations of the subject to the world as natural. But such an ideology can also mobilise around another conception of natural which is oppositional to that of dominant ideological forms.

In the case of migrant groups, class position (both in country of origin and country of migration) and ethnicity coexist and intersect to produce concrete effects. The state and the economic structure provide the arena for the dynamic interplay of class and ethnicity. Ethnicity may be used to mobilise power so that access to the state and to the achievement of the economistic aims of migration may be achieved. Since ethnicity is relational and oppositional its effects are greatest when there is competition for scarce resources or where different symbolic universes contest over claims to dominance.

Both ethnicity and class identity are situational and contextual. Ethnicity can act to create contradictions in class position and either blur class differences within the group or highlight class differences between ethnic groups. In this way both ethnicity and class can affect the acquisition, maintenance and distribution of wealth, prestige and political power.

The mode of struggle of migrants is often underplayed in the literature. Another facet that is often missing is that migrants are already class subjects before migration and the forms of exclusion they face in the society of migration are compounded by their class as well as their migrant status and racialisation. It is therefore necessary to consider the conditions under which migrants enter the economy and polity in relation to their constitution in the country of origin as well as the conditions they face in the country of migration. The following chapter will therefore focus on economic and ethnic relations under Colonialism in Cyprus in order to contextualise Greek-Cypriots in British society.

3 Contextualising Greek-Cypriots in economic and ethnic relations in Cyprus

Introduction

This chapter attempts to understand the nature of economic and ethnic relations in Cypriot society as a contextualising exercise for the study of Greek–Cypriot migrants in British society. Section I focuses on economic processes in Cyprus under British Colonial Rule. Section II looks at the nature of ethnic relations in Cyprus and the articulation of ethnicity, nationalism and class relations. This contextualising is necessary because migrants possess ethnic and class identities prior to their insertion into the society of migration, although these identities are constantly transformed.

Cyprus is a classic case of a small island with no intrinsic interest for colonialism which has suffered continuous colonisation. The history of the island is one of constant foreign rule by Myceneans, Assyrians, Egyptians, Persians, Romans, Lusignans, Venetians, Turks and Britons. A determining factor has been the geographical position of Cyprus in the Eastern Mediterranean which has made it a strategically desirable possession.

The island has a predominantly Greek–Orthodox and Greek speaking population (80 per cent or about 600,000 prior to 1974) who share a 'Hellenic' culture with mainland Greece, although developing a distinct Cypriot dialect and tradition. A further 18 per cent of the island has been Muslim and Turkish speaking (although since 1974, about 60,000 settlers have been brought in from the Turkish mainland to the Northern part of the island). There is also a scattering of Armenians, Maronites and others.

In 1571, when the Ottomans captured Cyprus from the Venetians, they introduced a Turkish Cypriot presence. Sultan Selim granted fiefs to about 20,000 or so Turkish soldiers who were added to by the Ottoman practice of shifting populations. The Byzantine period (AD 300–1192) had so entrenched the bonds of mainland Greece with the Cyprus periphery that the subsequent insertion of European feudalism and Ottoman rule failed to nullify the Greek cultural presence.

Britain was leased the island in 1878 and it was formally annexed at the Treaty of Lausanne in 1923, to be finally made 'independent' in 1960. Subsequently, a series of political events led to the Turkish invasion of

1974 and the annexation of 40 per cent of Cyprus territory by Turkey who have declared a separate Turkish Republic of Cyprus.

SECTION I

The Economic Context

Apart from introducing a Turkish speaking population to Cyprus, Ottoman rule had two additional effects. Firstly the Greek Orthodox Church was given a position of dominance through the Millett system which recognised the autonomy of different communities. This was after a period (of approximately 500 years) of having its economic and political power usurped. Under the Ottomans, its property was re-established and added to through the empowerment to exact religious fees and the practice of receiving donations from the peasantry.

In 1929 the Church held 6.8 per cent of the best agricultural land in the form of large estates which contrasted with the fragmentation common to Cypriot agricultural holdings. By 1960 the proportion held was 8-10 per cent (Meyer and Vassiliou, 1962). The Church was granted rights to collect taxes on behalf of the Ottomans and also become the political representative of the Greek Orthodox population. In this way its power base was established.

Secondly, Ottoman rule during its later phase fostered the development of trade and the growth of a local merchant class. The Sultan gave trading rights under privileged conditions to European powers and foreign consulates were established in Limassol. In 1821 tax farmers (local middlemen) were appointed and they tended to have links with foreign consulates. Corruption and tax extortion facilitated their entry into the wine and cereal trade.

Cyprus was leased to Britain in 1878. Britain introduced a stable money currency, tax farming was abolished and the government took over the collection of taxes. This gave rise to hostility as it reduced the power of the local trading class (who were also tax farmers). The money economy forced peasants to transform surplus into cash in order to pay the taxes exacted by the government. It also led to the growth of markets on a daily basis. Previously local animal and produce marketing took place two or three times a year at the Panegyria (religious festivals).

The money currency facilitated the growth of a money-lending class (tokoglyfous) who tided peasants over in times of poor harvest. Exorbitant interest rates were often exacted in kind from produce yielded by the following year's harvest. This placed the peasant in the debt (ipohreosi) of the merchant and also gave the merchant the right to buy produce at an exchange rate that he could fix. Abuses were frequent and greater indebtedness resulted which could lead to bankruptcy and the forced sale of land at the 'demoprasia' (the local auction). Surridge (1930) notes that the largest numbers of debtors were the poorer peasants. In the case of bankruptcy, there was no alternative but to seek employment in wage-labour by migrating to the town to work in building, the mines or petty crafts. Migration to Australia and England was also an opening that many took in the 1920s and 1930s, although mass migration to England did not take place till the middle 1950s.

Those who benefitted from the forced sale of land were quite frequently the creditors themselves who bought at a cheap price or those villagers with surplus cash who tended to be the largest land–holders. Some property would be bought back eventually by peasants. Merchants were unlikely to re–invest their capital in the agricultural sphere which remained technologically backward and labour intensive. Instead they invested in education for their sons.

A factor in the alienation from land was the locus of habitat – the urban environment – which made supervision of agricultural production difficult. Trade and marketing were also more potentially profitable. Carobs were the preferred staple crop but these, as with olives and almonds, could be kept and the land they stood on sold.

Various writers have claimed that British rule was instrumental in the development of nationalism in Cyprus and the creation of inter–ethnic conflict, and I shall examine the development of ethnicity in the following section. What is clear, however, is that colonialism in Cyprus took a primarily political form. It was rule for strategic purposes that was dominant as Sir Ronald Storrs (ex Governor of Cyprus) says in his autobiography:

England occupied Cyprus for strategic and imperial purposes (1945: 463).

Nonetheless, colonialism sought to exploit the colony economically while at the same time seeking, in paternalist fashion, to improve the social and 'moral' standards of its inhabitants. In Cyprus, it would be wrong to argue that the colonial leaders were only intent on economic exploitation for they improved communications, built roads, attempted to provide irrigation to solve the perpetual drought problem and so on. Road improvements were clearly linked to the needs of the colonialists for effective road networks to be used for strategic purposes. According to Jenness (1962: 162), the roadwork system was the main positive contribution of Britain.

In addition, Britain encouraged the development of credit cooperative societies, partly to control the power of the internal Greek–Cypriot bourgeoisie who they clashed with (there were many grievances over preferential economic treatment being given to external as opposed to indigenous capital). However, the credit cooperative societies mitigated to some extent the dependence of the Cypriot peasant on the merchant broker for tiding him over in times of poor harvest. Debts were rife in Cyprus until the 1950s, however (Meyer and Vassiliou, 1962). This was linked to the fragmentation of property which resulted from the bilateral inheritance system (involving transmission of property to children at marriage). The natural and ecological conditions of Cyprus such as draughts, poor soil, inadequate irrigation and the added lack of mechanised methods and technological advancement, contributed to rural indebtedness. The early years of the century saw some agricultural expansion but Jenness (1962) notes that lack of foreign trade, low prices and heavy taxation which:

> deprived peasants and merchants alike of any surplus that might have been used for trading ventures (:162).

The dominant economic issues during the first 50 years of British rule were the 'Tribute' and taxation. The 'Tribute' arose out of an agreement between Britain and Turkey to pay the latter a rent which it extracted from the Cypriot population. Churchill in 1907 stated:

> I had not realised that we have drawn from this island, exhausted as it was by 300 years of Turkish mismanagement, upwards of £1,800,000.

During the period 1878–1931, Greek Cypriot demands included a desire for ENOSIS (Union with Greece) which had been fired by the Greek struggle for Independence and the return to Greece of other primarily Greek speaking islands, However, they also contained demands for social reform, political representation and constitutional change. Poverty was rife in Cyprus and Sir Ronald Storrs (1945) says that after 50 years of British rule, 'Cyprus is in truth deadly poor' (: 491).

The 'Tribute' was a continual source of discontent, debilitating the peasantry and was later discovered to be extracted for fraudulent purposes. In fact it never reached Turkey but was taken by the British treasury. When it was abolished in 1927 by Sir Ronald Storrs, the British government imposed taxation for the so-called 'Defence of Cyprus'.

The 1929 Memorial by the Greek–Cypriot members of the Legislative Council contained complaints also concerning the advantages conferred to British capital as opposed to local Cypriot capital. One particular illustration of these advantages is found in the policy of importing from England goods that at times were in abundance locally.

Agriculture was still 'the basis of the economy of Cyprus' according to the Cyprus Government Annual Colonial Report for 1950. The outstanding fact of Cyprus agriculture however was that

> it provides the farmer with a very poor standard of living and it no longer produces enough to feed the island's population, still less to pay for its other essential needs (Government Census Report for 1946).

In 1946 the total farm population was 245,000 who formed 71 per cent of the total rural population, or 55 per cent of the total population of the island. The area of land cultivated in 1955 was still only 12 per cent (Meyer and Vassiliou, 1962), and as late as 1946 there were still 23,604 primitive threshing floors in use. In addition during this period only 3.5 per cent of the arable land was irrigable all year round (Government Census Report, 1950). While conditions in Cyprus in the 20th Century, in the villages, were still not very different from what they had been for the last

3,000 years, there occurred between 1881 and 1960 a trebling of the population from 186,173 to 576,566 (Republic of Cyprus 1977: 31).

There was considerable underemployment in Cyprus which was related to the mode of agricultural production and the failure to fully utilise natural resources. Important in this was the policy of importing goods and discouraging local-based industries. Rural unemployment was often as high as 30 per cent (Meyer and Vassiliou, 1962). A large section of labour was employed in military works, in the mines and in building, where employment was uncertain. Military works, for example, were not of a permanent nature and mines involved industrial methods which would replace unskilled labour. There was both rural overpopulation and a scarcity of skilled labour as technical education was not fostered (Persianis, 1971).

There was virtually no industry in Cyprus prior to World War II. According to Meyer and Vassiliou (1962):

> The copper mines, a few bottling plants and a handful of construction enterprises make up the island's industrial sector (: 43).

Between 1950-1958, mining and quarrying production grew by 31 per cent, construction 69 per cent, production of gas, electricity and water 800 per cent and manufacturing 11.9 per cent. By 1960, industrial production accounted for 25 per cent of the national income, mining accounting for one half of this and manufacturing and construction accounting for the other half (Meyer and Vassiliou, 1962: 38).

The tremendous expansion of construction works came from:

> the urban housing shortages created by World War II, military base construction, post war Government development programmes investing in roads and public utilities and the need for buildings of all kinds which accompanied the burgeoning of the island's 6 district towns (Meyer and Vassiliou, 1962: 43).

In relation to manufacturing, by 1954 there were 11,000 industrial enterprises, of which 94 per cent were small employing four persons or less.

However, by 1960, farming still accounted for over 50 per cent of economic activity and produced 25 per cent of the Cyprus national income. It is clear that economic conditions in Cyprus were improving by the 1950s, although rural problems of underemployment were prevalent and the economic disruption brought about by the political events after 1955 and the political and economic uncertainty with Independence in 1960 all played a part in spurring migration during this period.

SECTION II

The Development of Ethnicity in Cyprus

One of the outstanding features of ethnic relations on Cyprus has been what appear to be essential ethnic divisions and conflicts between the Greek–Cypriot population (who constitute 80 per cent approximately of the total) and the Turkish Cypriot population (of approximately 18 per cent). This conflict has been usually conceived in terms of an interaction between two distinct cultures and religions and a historical antagonism between them. For example the Turkish invasion of Cyprus in 1974 has often been explained in terms of the failure of Turks and Greeks to coexist or the economic oppression of Turks by Greeks (Attalides, 1977a). It is important therefore to examine the construction of Greek–Cypriot ethnicity historically.

This section considers the development of Greek–Cypriot ethnicity in a colonialist context. It particularly examines nationalist and class politics in Cyprus, their contradictory articulation and the formation of interethnic conflict. The following discussion will analyse the way in which ethnicity was dynamically and situationally constituted in Cyprus. It also provides essential background information on the constituent elements of the Greek–Cypriot ethnicity that migrants bring to Britain.

Greek–Cypriot ethnicity found a nationalist expression in opposition to British nationalism and Turkish–Cypriot ethnicity. It also found a culturalist and political expression as an identification with Hellenism.

Greek–Cypriot and Turkish–Cypriot Relations

Greek–Cypriots constituted, up to 1914, approximately 80 per cent of the population, the rest being mainly Turkish–Cypriot, with a scattering of Armenians, Maronites and others. It has been argued that some of the population shifted by the Ottomans to Cyprus were Christians originally and possibly of Greek origin (Papadopoulos, 1965). In addition it has been demonstrated that neither the ethnic or religious composition of the population which was shifted to Cyprus, nor the size, can explain the numbers who comprised the Moslem community from the 16th century onwards. During the early years of Ottoman rule, conversions from Christianity to Islam appear to have been fairly widespread, those who converted being then treated as full Ottoman citizens by the Turkish rulers. In this way, they avoided the exorbitant tax rates that Christians were subjected to and the social and economic disadvantages that they suffered.

Additional evidence is the presence of whole Moslem villages where inhabitants spoke only Greek, and the case of 'linobambakoi' (linen–cotton or crypto–Christians) who as time went by reverted to Christianity. The reversal generally took place during the British occupation of Cyprus (which began in 1878). In addition to the demographic fluctuation and interchangeability of Christian and Moslem (the dominant categories used rather than Greek and Turk), the number of mixed villages in Cyprus until the 1963 intercommunal riots testify to what has been termed 'traditional coexistence' (Kitromilides, 1977). What distinguished the two groups were religious beliefs and practices, their familial and social life and the low degree of intermarriage, although there is some evidence for the latter taking place.

More importantly, solidary bonds existed between Moslems and Christians. There were indeed families who included both Moslem and Christians due to the conversion process. But the bonds were mainly structured by the common economic conditions of peasants. This is indicated by a number of peasant revolts under Christian or Muslim leaders, which involved members from both faiths.

In 1764 Muslims and Christians came together to kill the new governor of Cyprus, Chil Osman in response to a decision to double taxation (Hill, 1952 Vol 4 :152-165). Sir George Hill mentions a 'common mob' in the 19th century in 1830 and 1833. Muslims and Christians often shared religious shrines. They also shared customs and traditions such as celebrating religious feasts and marriages. A Greek-Cypriot dialect also evolved that incorporated many Turkish words and was spoken by Christians and most Moslems (Pollis, 1973).

Extremely important within this pattern of coexistence are economic processes and structures. The merchant intermediary relation to the peasant producer was crucial. For what tied both Christian and Moslem together was their relation to merchant middlemen who supplied credit and provided marketing outlets.

Peasant producers relied on credit to tide them over in times of poor yield or until the crop was harvested and sold. Interest rates were high, corruption was widespread and merchants often claimed repayment by seizing part of the crop. Through the existence of a patronage power relation, political control of peasants was also established. According to Attalides (1979), this system still existed in 1974 when there were Greek-Cypriot intermediaries buying from Turkish-Cypriot peasants, although this could not have been widespread owing to the effective withdrawal of economic interaction in 1963 and the establishment of a practice within the Turkish-Cypriot enclaves of a from Turk to Turk economic policy.

Another economic link was through the sharecropping system, whereby spare land was combined with another family's spare labour, for shared production. In addition, up to fairly recently, in some cases 1974, Turkish and Greek-Cypriots patronized the same coffee house.

One significant effect of Ottoman rule, apart from the introduction of a Moslem community to Cyprus, was the restoration of the Greek Orthodox church to a position of political dominance within the Christian community, through the 'Millet' system. This granted the autocephalous Archbishop of Cyprus ecclesiastical and lay jurisdiction over the population. According to Pollis (1973:584) 'the communal nature of group relatedness was along religious lines' and not linked to notions of nationality or nationalism under the Ottomans.

The Development of Nationalism

In 1878, Cyprus was ceded to the British by the Cyprus Convention, annexed in 1914 and formally annexed at the Lausanne Conference in 1923. It has been argued that the onset of British rule gave the necessary impetus to the development of nationalism, especially amongst the Greek–Cypriot population in Cyprus (Pollis, 1973). However, it would be overstating the case to see the British administrative procedures as the sole elements in such a development. It is the way nationalist ideology was harnessed to the anti–colonialist struggle that is mainly responsible for the development of the Greek–Cypriot variant of nationalism.

One ingredient in the constitution of this variant was the introduction into Cyprus of the religious and chauvinist fanaticism of the 'Great Idea' (Megali Idea) , which sought for the restoration to Greece of all Greek-speaking lands and which was propagated by the Church and the internal bourgeoisie.

When Greece was freed from the Ottoman yoke after the prolonged Greek War of Independence of 1821, Greek Cypriot religious leaders began to express the desire to merge with the 'Motherland'. However, until 1878 and the onset of British rule, religious or linguistic differences defined the boundaries of the community. Under British Rule, the Church ceased to be the political representative of the Greek–Orthodox population and secular rule became established.

The growth of nationalism, expressed in the desire for Enosis and the desire for freedom from the Colonial yoke of the British was during the early years of British rule articulated mainly by the Church leaders and a few members of the newly emerging merchant elite, and did not penetrate to other sections of the population. Early nationalism of a more secular form is linked to the growth of elites desiring to guarantee their local power base in the struggle against the colonial centre. The main antagonism was between two elite groups, the British administrators and the local merchant class. This was to some extent linked to the growth of a modern state with its central administrative structure which vitiated rule by the local political leaders. It also grew out of the ability of certain local political groups to play off the state and the local political scene in their own interests. This was related to a strong power base, advantageous access to local resources, the distribution of commodities, the use of patronage and terrorisation of the peasantry.

The latter took two forms. Firstly, the peasantry, under the ideological leadership of the Church, could be threatened with the withdrawal of religious guidance and support. Secondly, under the economic and political rule of the merchant intermediary it was materially terrorised into support. Equally important however, was the cultural hegemony of the 'intellectuals', the priest, the teacher and the merchant, whom the peasants looked to for ideological guidance. The local power base of the merchant, in coalition with the Church, was dependent on the control of external marketing and credit networks rather than the control of the means of production.

Nationalism, at the beginning of the 20th Century, was spread by the Church through its spiritual leadership and also through its control of the only forms of schooling, the religious instruction given to children. The Church's renewed nationalistic activities were linked partly to the diminution of it's role under British rule which secularised the state.

Enosis as a mass movement was not to emerge until the 1940s and 1950s. Before considering the factors that contributed to this, it is important to examine in more detail further aspects of British rule that facilitated the growth of ethnicity and nationalism.

Constitutional Factors in the Development of Ethnicity

When Britain assumed the administration of Cyprus in 1878 it began with the assumption (as it has been claimed it did for its other multi–ethnic and multi–religious colonies) that each of the Cypriot communities had diverse interests and aspired to separate development (Van Coufoudakis, 1976). This was reinforced by the quick representation made by Church leaders for union with Greece. The first British High Commissioner (Sir Garnet Wolseley) was met in 1878 by the Bishop of Citium with the words:

> We accept the change of Government inasmuch as we trust that Great Britain will help Cyprus, as it did the Ionian Islands, to be united with Mother Greece, with which it is naturally connected (Luke, 1957).

Already then, before the onset of British rule, we find the desire to unite with Greece, for Enosis (Union with Greece). This was predicated on the Megali Idea, the panhellenic ideology which involved the dream that the Byzantine empire would again be recreated, and which included Cyprus amongst its irredentist claims. The nationalism it purveyed was chauvinistic, romantic–idealist, thrived on the mythology of a glorious Hellenic past, and was aimed at the aggrandisement of the Hellenic world. It's most forceful purveyors were the Church, and after the 1940s (with the growth of left syndicalism and Communism in Cyprus) it had an explicitly anticommunist character.

The particular development of the ideology of Enosis was partly structured by the policy of the British colonial power. The political system that the British introduced by the 1882 constitution was founded, in fact, on the assumption of persistent ethnic conflict, formalised ethnic divisions and was conducive to laying the seeds for bi–national consciousness.

The bonds that had developed between Muslims and Christians under the Ottoman empire, crumbled to a large extent under British rule. Each of the communities was endowed with certain national attributes and regarded as a 'natural extension of Greece and the Ottoman Turks respectively' (Pollis, 1972).

This is particularly clear in the constitutional structure. In the legislative Council each newly constructed 'ethnic' group (Muslims now becoming 'Turks') was given proportional representation, always guaranteeing the dominance of the British authority. There were nine Greek Cypriot members, three Turkish-Cypriot and six British members. An alliance between the Turkish-Cypriot and British members could be off-set against the Greek-Cypriot members (Orr, 1918). The latter express their grievances in a Memorial of 1929:

> A foremost and basic complaint ... being kept separated from their Mother Country, Greece, with whom sacred and unbreakable ties of blood, religion, language, traditions and national conscience link them together.

In addition there is much dissatisfaction with the Legislature and its practices, especially the 'King's' right to legislate for the Colony by order in Council. The document defines the Turkish-Cypriot community as a 'Small Turkish Minority'. There are also economic grievances, the main one being 'the excessive amount of taxation and its proportion to the gross production', the numbers and pay of the Civil Service and the injustice of the 'so-called' Tribute (Memorial 1929:8).

The Constitution, as well as writing in inter-communal divisions at the political representation level, also expanded and segregated the educational system, each community being dependent for personnel and literature on mainland Greece or Turkey (Van Coufoudakis, 1975). In addition it allowed the communities the freedom to fly Greek or Turkish flags. This exacerbated already existing group differences and fostered national political elites protecting the 'interests' of their own communities.

Enosis – the Form of Greek-Cypriot Nationalism

The form that Greek-Cypriot nationalism took under British rule was expressed in mass political action for the first time in the 'great October events' of 1931, when the Governor's house in Nicosia was burnt down. This led to the instigation of direct rule and the abandonment of the Constitution. The main disturbances were immediately aroused by the economic conditions of the Cypriot people, especially the imposition of crippling taxation. (Cyprus Pocket Book, 1956). They were, however, led by the Church although the young Communist Party of Cyprus (KKK-Kommounistikon Komma Kyprou), formed in 1926, was also implicated, some of its leading members being indeed outlawed or exiled (Anthias and Ayres, 1983). This was a small contingent of men, mainly politicised through the experiences of the 1914-1919 war, some educated in Greece and influenced greatly by the October Revolution in Tsarist Russia in 1917. The failure of the Communist movement, which was to ascend in social and political significance in the following years, to rally economic and anti-colonial discontent under it's own wing, is very significant (Anthias and Ayres, 1983).

It has been argued that Enosis was a social movement which was founded on chauvinist ideological constituents and was aimed at the aggrandisement of the Hellenic World. The material conditions of Enosis must be located in the extreme economic exploitation and oppression of the Cypriot peasantry. The merchants and the intermediaries had their

42

own interests in fighting colonial rule, for the British colonialists clearly privileged British capital, at the expense of local capital. The Greek Legislative Council was mainly composed of this class. Sir Ronald Storr, noted that in 1926, of the Greek members, 8 were advocates (3 of them moneylenders, one landowner/moneylender), one was a bishop, one was a merchant and one was a farmer (Storrs, 1943). The merchants and professionals who sat in the Colonial Legislative Council came into conflict over the financial relationship between Cyprus and Britain and the expansion of constitutional powers to the British. One specific grievance was that English companies were exempted from paying duty for importing foreign materials and goods which were in abundance locally. Another was that privileged facilities were provided for British companies but denied to Cypriot ones (Memorial, 1929). Since the Council was limited in its powers, the Church became the agency for the pursuit of its interests and an alliance grew between the bourgeoisie and church leaders.

The bourgeoisie could readily take to an ideology fostered by the Church which was based on elitist and reactionary elements, specially since Enosis would facilitate their growth as a bourgeois class unhampered by a colonial power which disadvantaged it. It is interesting that British capital in this instance did not seek for the co-operation of local capital.

The failure to lay the seeds of a compradore bourgeoisie during this period have been linked to Britain's ability to manipulate ethnic divisions for its own interests. The peasantry, on the other hand, were at the mercy of the merchant intermediary class. In expressing its opposition to this class, the British sought to appeal to the peasantry through the encouragement of credit co-operative societies. However, the failure to ease the crippling colonial taxation prevented an alliance with the Peasantry who were also being hit by the crisis of the World Economy of the 1930s. The economic discontent found expression in anti-colonialist and nationalist sentiments in the 1931 riots. Thus anti-colonialism and nationalism were firmly married in the consciousness and political action of the Greek-Cypriot peasant and working class. Enosis, despite the chauvinism and racism of its specific formulation by the Church leaders and the bourgeoisie also contained within it national-liberationist and anti-colonialist tendencies which were to achieve their full contradictory expression and subsequent subordination within the National-Liberation struggle of 1955 to 1960.

Enosis in the 1940s' was the official ideology of the Church and internal bourgeoisie but became the dominant constituent of Greek-Cypriot ethnic consciousness. Its component parts were the following:

a) A resurrection and amplification of a Hellenistic 'Megali Idea' tradition – in counterposition to Ottoman Turks (for this was forged in Greece under Ottoman Rule and in opposition to it). This was an affirmation of 'Greekness' as an opposition to 'Turkishness' or 'heathenism', which embodied the notion of a 'Christian-Hellene'. Religious sentiments were integral to this and the equation of Greek-Orthodoxy with the conception of nationhood is important. Linguistic nationalism was also present; it was a unification of all Greek speaking and Greek Orthodox lands that was proposed. A 'Graikos' was a Hellenic, Greek–speaking, Christian Orthodox.

b) Enosis was also formulated as a national liberationist political ideal and was increasingly articulated in opposition to British rule. The British were neither Greek–speaking nor Christian Orthodox and were indeed economic exploiters, preventing the development of the local economy, and political oppressors. Thus Enosis involved the contradiction of a reactionary chauvinist element (postulating the superiority of a Greek cultural tradition) and an incipient radical anti–imperialism and struggle against economic exploitation. What Greek–Cypriots opposed was the enforced and economically exploitative rule of a foreign bourgeoisie and of foreign capital. This was indeed to find expression in socialist discourse (Anthias and Ayres, 1983). However, although Enosis was national-liberationist, in as much as it sought the freedom of Cyprus from British colonial rule, it nevertheless sought encompassment under the rule of another nation–state (Greece). The conception of national freedom thus differs from that of most nationalist movements which are secessionist.

c) Ethnic consciousness in Cyprus was able, at the popular level, to articulate class elements, while at the same time it constructed a natural national Greek unity. This link was forged with the development of the Progressive Movement in Cyprus, which was able to see national liberation as a first stage of the class struggle against the international bourgeoisie.

Ethnic Conflict

In terms of political practice there can be no doubt concerning the disastrous effects of the Enosis movement in the development of ethnic conflict and the growth of a polarised bi–nationalism in Cyprus. In the 1940s there grew a concomitant Turkish–Cypriot nationalism fostered by Turkish extremist elements but also as a response to the form that the Enosis movement was taking. There was no attempt to incorporate the Turkish–Cypriots into the National–Liberation struggle.

Turkish–Cypriot anti–Enosists had existed in the early part of this century but they came mainly from the Turkish–Cypriot urban elite who favoured the continuation of British Rule. In December 1949, 15,000 Turkish Cypriots marched through the Turkish quarter of Nicosia, in opposition to Enosis. It appears that it was not, however, until 1955 that the Turkish national cry for Partition or Taksim took off as a main Turkish–Cypriot demand (The Tripartite Conference on the Eastern Mediterranean and Cyprus, held in London on 29th August 1955, formally introduced Turkey into the dispute and recognised her claims on Cyprus).

The notion of Partition was the full expression of Turkish–Cypriot ethnicity but had in fact been raised formally in 1956 by the British who led the argument for double self determination. Britain encouraged Turkey's claim to Cyprus (renounced in 1923 at the Lausanne Conference) in order to contain Greek and Greek–Cypriot pressures and by emphasising the important strategic needs of the Western alliances. Turkish Cypriot nationalism was also purveyed by the Turkish Cypriot educational system manned and organised through Turkey. In 1924, Headlam Morlay, the official British historian could write:

> The Mahometan population, being as they were a minority regarded British rule as a safeguard and accepted the new situation (Annexation) showing no tendency to identify themselves with the Turks (Kyrris, 1977:37).

By 1948, however, Turkish–Cypriot leaders were demanding the return of Cyprus to Turkey:

> its previous suzerain and nearest neighbour and in a better position than any other neighbouring state to defend it (Hill, 1952, vol 4: 563–564).

The activities of the British during the 1955–59 EOKA struggle helped to cement even further inter–communal divisions. The British encouragement of partition has already been mentioned. In addition, Britain used large numbers of Turkish–Cypriots as auxiliary policemen and specially trained commandoes during this 'Emergency period' (Kyrris, 1977:46). More significantly, by 1958, Turkish–Cypriot nationalists, possibly under the direction and pay of the Colonial government, began terrorist activities with their organisation, T.M.T. According to Kyrris (1977), a considerable number of Turkish–Cypriot auxiliary policemen were members and collaborated with the local agents of the British Intelligence Service.

The British in 1955 had allowed the formation of Kucuks party – 'The Cyprus is Turkish Party'. The activities of the T.M.T. and the Turkish–Cypriot auxiliaries were directed against both Greek–Cypriots and Turkish–Cypriots. T.M.T. in 1958 began a campaign of terror against left progressive and democrat Turks, making for example, on 22nd May, a murder attempt against Ahmet Sati, Secretary of the Turkish section of PEO, two days later killing Fazil Ontour Sellar, a progressive Turkish–Cypriot journalist and soon afterwards Ahmet Yiahia and Ahmet Ibrahim. This campaign of terror forced most Turkish Cypriot workers to leave PEO and AKEL, many either emigrating or joining the Turkish Trade Union. At this same time eight Greek residents of the village 'Kontemenos' were brutally killed. Throughout 1957 and 1958 the Anglo Turkish co–operation in Cyprus was promoted, the number of Turkish Cypriots employed as policemen rising. Nicosia had been divided in 1956, further violence breaking out between Turkish and Greek–Cypriots 'proving' that the two communities could not live together, as Kucuk, the Turkish Cypriot leader declared in January 1958.

Ethnic divisions and conflicts were thus structured by the growth of the Enosis movement, the utilisation of Turkish–Cypriots to counter Greek–Cypriot demands by the British, the increasing bringing in of Ankara and the interests of Turkey into the dispute and the development of Turkish–Cypriot nationalism and claims for Taksim (Partition). Enosis and Taksim stood in opposition as the representation of Greek–Cypriot and Turkish–Cypriot ethnicity. These ethnic divisions were further to be exacerbated by the Independence agreements of 1959–60 (Zurich agreement). The struggle involved the crystallisation of both ethnic and political/class conflicts. It took the form of ethnic struggle between rightist elements of both Communities (EOKA and TMT) but also class struggle of the right against the left (EOKA against AKEL and TMT against Turkish progressives). The class element and ethnic element were combined in opposition to British rule, anti–colonialism being an expression of nationalism/ethnicity and of class. Despite the ideology of EOKA leaders, however, the fighters were mainly from the working class. Markides (1977) has shown that they were indeed both urban and young. 77 per cent of those who were outlawed by the police during 1955–59 were 15–25 years old and so were 87.2 per cent of those brought to trial, 32.1 per cent were high school students and the rest were young technicians, carpenters, mechanics and electricians. These were, on the whole, migrants to towns with only elementary education. Markides characterises EOKA as an urban guerilla movement relying on sabotage. Most of the clashes were carried out in urban areas, significant since according to the Census of 1960, Cyprus was only 35.9 per cent urban and 64.1 per cent rural. Their active support, however, came from the anti–communist national bourgeoisie.

In order to further understand the polarised ethnicity in Cyprus the next section considers the political solution imposed by the Zurich–London Agreement of 1959.

Constitutional Factors in the Growth of Ethnic Conflict

It was the Greek and Greek–Cypriot fears of partition that brought Greece and Turkey together at Zurich in February 1959. The dominant roles played by Britain, Greece and Turkey in the independence talks that were to form the basis of the constitution and related treaties ensured that their interests were represented. The ability to 'resolve' the Cyprus issue in the interests of NATO was made easier by internal developments on the island, which had led to the growth of ethnicity and ethnic conflict.

Firstly, the Zurich–London agreement established the form of the constitution of the Republic of Cyprus and set up three treaties allowing the retention of colonial rule albeit in a different form (Windsor, 1964:3). Britain was to retain 99 square miles of Cyprus territory and 32 other points all over Cyprus and established two military bases in the South – overall retaining 3 per cent of the island through the Treaty of Establishment. The Treaty of Guarantee prohibited either Union or Partition and states:

> In the event of a breach of the provision of the present treaty, Greece, Turkey and the UK undertake to consult together with respect to the representation or measures necessary to ensure observance of these provisions. In so far as common or concerted action may not prove possible each of the three guaranteeing

powers reserve the right to take action with the sole aim of re-establishing the state of affairs created by the present Treaty (HMSO, 1960).

This was to allow Turkey in 1974 to invade Cyprus on just such a pretence. The Treaty of Alliance provided for a permanent presence of Greek and Turkish troops on the island, initially comprising 950 Greek and 650 Turkish soldiers and also set up a tripartite headquarters (with Cyprus) to control military contingents on the island. This Treaty of Guarantee especially linked Constitutional developments in Cyprus to the interests of the Guarantor powers for they could intervene if they believed that the state of affairs created by the Treaty had been changed. In addition the development of a Cypriot ethnic consciousness was made almost impossible by the legitimation of separate Greek and Turkish ethnicity through their military presence. This Treaty also had the significant effect of formally re-establishing Turkish rights in Cyprus ceded in 1923.

The development of neo-colonial rule as opposed to colonialism requires the transfer of state authority into indigenous hands. In classical form, this involves indigenous entrepreneurs being 'compradores' i.e. intermediaries between foreign interest and the indigenous polity and economy and-or turning to the state as a source of both capital and contracts. In Cyprus it was a matter more of the centrality of political rule for preserving the interests of the Western Alliances and international capital. Although formal internal state power was passed to indigenous hands, the three treaties curtailed the autonomy of local developments and gave right of interference to three foreign powers, extending colonial domination thus from one state to three.

The Constitution of 1960 established thoroughgoing bi-communalism in all spheres and all levels of government (Kyriakides, 1968:58). The Turkish Cypriots (18 per cent of the population) were given 30 per cent parliamentary representation with 15 out of 50 seats. The President was always to be 'Greek' and the Vice-President 'Turk' each elected by his own community, deriving their authority from each and responsible and accountable to them. Both had right of veto on foreign affairs, defense and security and could thus block decisions of the other. The Vice-President could never 'stand in' for the President, who if absent would delegate power to the President and Vice-President of the House of Representatives, who were always Greek and Turkish respectively.

A Council of Ministers was established, seven to be Greek and three to be Turkish owing allegiance to their respective communities.

Bicommunalism was also written into the Civil Service and security forces (70/30 Greek/Turkish) in the army (60/40) and at every level of Government and administration. The Constitution contained certain fundamental articles that 'cannot in any way be amended, whether by way of variation, addition or repeal. (Adams, 1966:486).

Clearly such constitutional provisions required a great deal of collaboration and agreement between the communal representatives to work. Within three years they had broken down, the Turkish Cypriots withdrawing from Government and forming Turkish–Cypriot enclaves. One of the problems was that Greek and Turkish Cypriot leaders conceptualised the Constitution in different ways, the Turkish–Cypriots endowing it with a federal character and seeing it as protecting their rights. They thus argued for its rigid implementation. Greek–Cypriots saw it as representing the interests of Turkey and other foreign nations and giving unfair representation to Turkish–Cypriots. They desired an integrated unitary state. In fact, Makarios, the first President of the Republic, still publicly expressed support for the Hellenic ideal which was hardly conducive to ethnic co–operation. The Turkish–Cypriots clung to their constitutional rights most tenaciously. The crunch came when President Makarios issued constitutional proposals to amend them, which led to inter–communal fighting, the entry of Turkish troops and the de facto withdrawal in 1963 of Turkish–Cypriots.

At the first Presidential elections Archbishop Makarios won a decisive victory largely through the public acclaim of his EOKA involvement. Makarios' 'patriotic front' was premised on the overall unity of interests of Greek Cypriots irrespective of ideological differences with the aim of building Greek–Cypriot strength to fight the constitutional structure of Zurich. Makarios' 'patriotic front' was thus premised on ethnic unity.

Between 1964 – 1974 the Turkish Cypriots were effectively partitioned, their economic position worsening in relation to that of the increasingly entrepreneurial Greek Cypriot community.

What indeed were the economic conditions of the Turkish Cypriots during this period? A glance at Turkish Cypriot and Greek Cypriot regions and dwellings clearly shows today a marked economic disadvantage. This is partly the result of developments since the 1960s with the economic policy of 'from Turk to Turk' within the Turkish Cypriot Community (Attalides, 1977a). The discussion of the conditions of the Turkish–Cypriots is important since the lack of differentiation, politically and economically, made their control by the TMT easier.

The economic position of Turkish Cypriots has historical roots. The Ottomans reserved military and administrative careers for themselves and Christians were for the first time since the 12th century allowed to enter trade. This was reinforced by the establishment of European consulates in Cyprus, who employed Greek–Christians who would then lend money to the peasantry. Thus the Cypriot bourgeoisie was mainly Greek and there were always more wealthy individuals within the Christian population than the Moslem.

In 1963 only 15 per cent of all car–owners were Turkish–Cypriot. In 1961, the average per capita income of Turkish–Cypriots was 20 per cent lower than for Greek–Cypriots. This reflected the higher number of commercial and professional workers who were Greek (Attalides, 1977a). It did not mean necessarily that a peasant or worker who was Turkish–Cypriot was poorer. Turkish–Cypriots also remained disproportionately concentrated in government employment. They were also more urban than Greek–Cypriots which is a result of their position under Ottoman rule as administrators and their subsequent orientation towards this. Under

British colonialism, Greek Cypriots developed commercially whereas Turkish Cypriots remained mainly peasants or administrators.

In 1974 EOKA(B) resurrected itself but this time with very little mass support and staged a fascist coup in collaboration with the Greek junta. Turkey invaded soon of afterwards and took over 40 per cent of Cypriot territory which it declared as an Independent Turkish Republic of Cyprus (using the Treaty of Guarantee as a legitimation for entering Cyprus).

Greek Cypriot Ethnicity – Concluding Remarks

Greek Cypriot ethnicity was defined in opposition to British Colonialism and to the Turkish ethnic category and the two were subsequently aligned. The form that ethnicity took was then to establish the hegemony of the Church leadership and internal bourgeoisie and undercut the expression of horizontal class alliances between the Greek–Christian and Moslem population.

Ethnicity in this instance can be seen to articulate class interests and anti–colonialism, but subsequently to obfuscate them through the submergence of the political representative of a class – the working class party – within the ethnic struggle. Ethnicity can thus be seen to have the ability to articulate different ideological discourses and to represent different class political interests. It can be harnessed to different political projects for it is essentially the ideological construction of an origin as a significant arena for struggle. This construction found expression in the fight against colonialism but also in identification with Hellenism via the hegemony of the Church and bourgeoisie which then allowed it to become directed towards a chauvinist nationalism, exemplified in Cyprus by the form that the ENOSIS movement took, especially in the EOKA struggle.

Events since 1974 in particular, have led to a decline of this nationalistic formulation. Most Greek–Cypriots believe that Turkey is unlikely to withdraw from Cyprus territory or to make many concessions and have reconciled themselves to some form of 'federal' solution. Despite this the articulation of Greek–Cypriot ethnicity in opposition to Turkish–Cypriot ethnicity has been reaffirmed by the presence of Turkey. On the other hand Greece is no longer constituted as the 'Motherland'. There was large scale disillusionment with Greece's unwillingness to actively help Greek Cypriots during the Turkish invasion. Increasingly Greek Cypriots see their ethnic position as 'Cypriot'. The development of a new Cypriot ethnicity in relation to all Cypriots including migrants is raised also.

In addition to the possibility of a new ethnicity in Cyprus, certain developments within the Turkish–occupied sector indicate that events could lead to less divisive relations between Turkish–Cypriots and Greek–Cypriots. Discontent within this sector is pronounced and Greek Cypriots are increasingly aware of the local–based opposition of Turkish–Cypriot workers to the Turkish militia and authority. In addition, Trade Unions from the two sectors, as well as youth organisations have established contact, which reaffirms the potential for less divisive ethnic relations in the future. Ironically, the 'imposed' solution of the so–called Cyprus problem has had one positive result in ringing the last toll-bell for ENOSIS and reaffirming the need for Cypriot unity on new and very different political and constitutional terms through some form of federation.

The form that ethnicity took, as an articulation of nationalist and anti-colonialist interests, can go part of the way in explaining the strength of the Cypriot 'ethnic' orientation and the lack of desire to be assimilated culturally to British society. However the maintenance of this ethnicity has also been facilitated by the continuing effectivity of the Cyprus problem. After the events of 1974 (the coup and subsequent Turkish invasion) a great deal of ethnic activity was generated in Britain and it served to re-ethnicise some of the younger generation.

However ethnicity is dynamic and cannot be explained purely with reference to the on-going effects of a construct originating elsewhere. Particular processes within British society, structuring the initial economic and social placement of Cypriots are extremely important and I shall consider them in the next chapter.

Two further points need to be made however concerning the political/national dimension – an ongoing one – for Greek Cypriots. One is that class discourse was contained in their ethnicity – via anti-colonialism and 'unjust' 'unfair', 'foreign' and 'monopoly' capital – and this defined the class enemy in ethnic terms (as British colonialist). This finds its contradictory expression within the consciousness of Greek-Cypriot migrants in Britain. Another point is related to the contents of the ethnic ideology, deriving from the mythology of a Hellenic cultural superiority and imbuing Greek-Cypriots with what they regard as a valuable cultural 'resource', their Greekness. However, in day-to-day terms this is often fired by the 'moral' trump-card of the Cypriot – the 'sanctity' of female sexual purity and the Cypriot family.

4 Exclusion and opportunity

Introduction

It used to be a well-held maxim that Southern European migrants to the United Kingdom did not present a 'problem' for the state or for the principle of social justice. These migrants were often studied in terms of their cultural adaptation or 'exotic' cultural presence in British society and issues of racism, or ethnic disadvantage were rarely explored (eg Dench 1977). This was partly the result of associating the fate of 'non-black' migrants to Britain with their American counterparts. John F Kennedy said, referring to the United States:

> We are all immigrants (Glazer, 1981: 7).

But as John Rex has pointed out, recent migrants to Britain:

> enter a system in which the native working class already exercises partial political control of its own welfare state system, so that the new migrants are seen as latecomers and outsiders and are thus more like colonial immigrants (Rex, 1981: 18).

Despite John Rex's reference, the issue of the commonality between white and black migrant groups in Britain is still rarely raised, the first being conceived as 'broadly successful' whereas the second may be depicted as a super-exploited sub-proletariat. This raises two issues. One is the issue of the heterogeneity of the migrant population. Can it be conceptualised merely in terms of a racial(ised) divide and if so what are the specific mechanisms by which racial ideology presents class effects? The second issue concerns indeed the extent to which class disadvantage can be understood in specific ethnic/racial terms, to what extent ethnic groupings constitute an underclass and what the mechanisms are by which this is assured.

A broadening of concern with ethnic disadvantage (as opposed to merely disadvantage structured by racial prejudice and discrimination) has been partly the result of the increase in migrant workers and their importance for European capitalism. Also there is increasing recognition of divisions within the 'Black' category and the existence of different forms of racism (Cohen & Bains, 1989).

On first view the discussion of Greek-Cypriots in the context of race and migrant labour theories may seem inappropriate. Firstly Greek Cypriots are at the common-sense or apparent level not a case of a colonial migrant population, as it has been usually implied if not consistently specified as 'black' or 'coloured'. However, a closer examination of the Cypriot case and of the theoretical premises involved may highlight some of the problems contained within the theories and their ambiguities. This also raises the issue of the nature and limits of 'blackness' since it never only refers to black skin as such and is often used to specify a unity of experience or as a political category.

Greek-Cypriots are a colonial migrant group. Cyprus was under the Colonial Rule of the British from 1878 to 1960. They formed part of the wave of New Commonwealth migration and have been experiencing the same re-definition of their status as other colonial migrants vis-a-vis Immigration Acts and the new Nationality Bill. Since a large number of theories which are concerned with the origin and effectivity of racial ideology posit the importance of colonialism in the structuring of ethnic relations, Cypriots will fit the rubric. If a separate sphere of 'black' colonial relations is posited then it is necessary to specify its distinct modality and trajectory. In addition the ongoing specificity of 'colour-racism' needs to be discussed (Anthias and Yuval-Davis, 1992).

Secondly, Greek-Cypriots also experience the kind of exclusion processes viz housing, employment and education (Swann, 1985) that so many reports on race relations have highlighted as working through the administrative procedures of allocation of resources or through lack of opportunities engendered by colonial underdevelopment, low skills and different cultural expectations. The case of Western European gastarbeiter populations, like the Turks in West Germany (Minority Rights Group Report 28 1978), shows that in times of economic recession feeling towards migrants becomes more hostile as they have been defined as outside the national boundary and therefore as not having a legitimate claim to resources like jobs, housing etc of the national collectivity. In Britain the exclusion exists not only against those who are defined as Black (a shifting boundary marker) but those whose language and cultural differences also define them as outside the national or ethnic boundary. Various writers on ethnicity have noted the importance of language and culture (eg Gellner, 1964) on the integration of the modern state. In Britain, as Glazer (1981) notes in 'The Ethnic Factor' there is concern over the transformation of the 'demographic balance' of the national collectivity, a concern shared by most national groupings and state (Anthias and Yuval-Davis, 1989).

To what extent are Greek-Cypriots and other minority groups similarly subjected to these processes and what are the differences and the reasons for these differences? One important factor may be competition by differently constructed 'ethnics' for scarce resources with the indigenous population. If Greek-Cypriots, like the Chinese, have removed themselves from the competitive arena then this may explain to some extent the lower degree of interpersonal hostility they may face.

At a different level racial differences are imbued with valuation and ideological/political manipulation at the level of dominant ideology and the State. These modes of ideological transmission via the media in particular are being challenged albeit in an inadequate and often contradictory fashion (Ball and Solomos 1991, Anthias and Yuval–Davis, 1992) by the whole race relations 'industry' that has grown up viz the CRE, the local CRCs and multi–ethnic and multi–cultural education programmes. While at one level the State attempts to challenge dominant racial mythologies on the other hand the legal/political framework through its immigration laws and the re–definition of citizenship rights legitimises them.

A pertinent question that is often asked in the literature is the extent to which 'cultural choice' can explain the employment, housing and educational location of migrant groups. In discussing these elements it is important to consider the relationship between exclusion practices and the forms of 'managing' these in terms of the ethnic resources a migrant group possesses. The contention here is that any 'cultural choice' has to be conceptualised in addition as a 'management strategy' vis–a–vis the disadvantages attending migrant or ethnic minority position (disadvantages that may vary for different ethnic groups) and not only in terms of a 'racialised' divide. In addition these disadvantages will vary for the different economic and sexual categories within any one ethnic group.

Employment

The jobs that Cypriots, like other migrants, took were those least attractive to the indigenous population. The jobs taken were those that required little language skills or where Cypriots could use their own skills in shoe–making, tailoring or dressmaking or the traditional sewing skills of their wives, sisters or mothers. In the early days, men did 'waiting' or worked in the kitchens and relied on working long hours and/or on good tips to save enough to bring over their wives and children. Many saved in order to set up small cafes, restaurants and factories. The early conditions in these small factories, in basements which were damp and cold, working day and night, are often quoted by migrants and were the subject of a series of articles in the London Greek–Cypriot paper Vema in the early 1950s. In the 1971 Census (the 1981 census does not provide supplementary tables linking employment and country of birth. The Labour Force Surveys on the other hand omit the Cypriot category) as in earlier Censuses, Cypriots were over–represented, compared to the general population, in the self–employed and small employer category and in semi–skilled and unskilled work. They were also under–represented in the non–manual categories. Cypriots are very under–represented in the professional category and present more in the skilled manual (40.8 per cent) compared to the N.C.W. total of 31.5 per cent for males (OPCS, 1971). Fewer were in the semi–skilled category and unskilled. Thus from this simple comparison we can say that they do not suffer the same degree overall of employment disadvantage. However, there are differences within the N.C.W. category that are significant and Indian migrants for example differ from those from Pakistan and the Caribbean especially in being very much more represented in the skilled non-manual category, intermediate and professional work. Black workers are sectorised also far more in different capital – engineering foundry, textiles and more of them are general labourers. Cypriots work lengthy hours in low-skilled work in small enterprises in the catering and service sectors. West Indians and Pakistanis on the other hand are more in the highly mechanised, heavily capitalised routinised and repetitive assembly line, often in 'local' firms of multi-national engineering plants and are subject to processes of deskilling and massification. West Indians are most likely to be in the vanguard of British industry in this sense (Hall et al, 1978: 349).

Different groups of Commonwealth immigrants were associated with different jobs in various areas of residence. For example, West Indians were associated with buses on London Transport and West Indian women with Catering. Indian and Pakistani men were associated with textiles in West Yorkshire and Indian women with clerical work. Cypriots, on the other hand were associated with self-employment or family businesses in the catering and clothing industries. Some of the literature on ethnicity and work tends to conceptualise these differences in terms of cultural 'choice' made by different migrant groups. Although it is true that Cypriots indeed make choices that are informed by cultural expectations, these are taken within a framework of migrant disadvantage. This disadvantage relates to the 'class' characteristics of migrants on entry and the way they are inserted into the social relations of the country of residence.

The issue of cultural 'choice' or structural disadvantage will be addressed later on in this chapter by looking at the tendency for Greek-Cypriots to be self-employed.

The main characteristics of Cypriot employment patterns are the following [1]. Firstly, Cypriot males show a marked leaning towards self-employment, 22.9 per cent of them being self-employed (including those with and without employees) compared to 9.3 per cent for the total British working population.

Secondly, in terms of occupation, Cypriot male workers are found mainly as service workers, the 1971 Census for example showing 22.6 per cent in this occupation, followed by 12 per cent as engineering and allied workers and 7 per cent as labourers. Of Cypriot women workers 30.5 per cent are clothing workers followed by 22.6 per cent as service workers and 20 per cent as clerical workers. There is some indication that younger Cypriot women are shifting away from clothing (where they are generally machinists or finishers) to clerical work. In addition, however, many Cypriot women work as homeworkers and this tends to be an unregistered working population. It has been estimated that in Haringey about 66 per cent of Cypriot women workers are clothing workers either in small dress-making factories (outdoor units supplied by large manufacturers) or at home.

The largest proportion of Cypriot male workers are skilled manual – this accounts for 40.8 per cent followed by the semi-skilled, accounting for 17.7 per cent. Professional Cypriots on the other hand are few, in 1971 being only 2.9 per cent of male workers and 0.3 per cent of female workers. In terms of Industry Orders, Cypriot men are found mainly in miscellaneous services where 41.1 per cent of them are self-employed followed by clothing where 28.5 per cent are self-employed and retail distribution where 47.4 per cent are self-employed.

An important feature of Cypriot employment which is concentrated mainly in the service sector, the clothing sector and retail distribution, is that this is characterised by small firms. For example, in the miscellaneous services the majority of men are 'service, sport and recreation workers' of which most are in the catering industry. Immigrants are crucial to the day-to-day survival of these firms for they generally work with low profit margins and are particularly vulnerable to economic fluctuations. They also usually involved poor working conditions, long hours and instability of employment. If we examine Cypriot employees in these industries, we find a tendency to work within Cypriot-owned firms. This has two effects. One is that it serves to maintain the ethnicity and insularity of Cypriots in relation to British society. This also clearly separates them from the political struggles of the working class as a whole. This insularity also allows them to remain ignorant of legislation which secures their rights as workers, like redundancy legislation, safety at work and pay regulations. Most Cypriot firms are characterised by the non-unionisation of the workforce and this clearly limits the ability of workers to fight for better pay and conditions. The lack of Cypriot unionisation is also related to the 'ideology of return' of Cypriots for they do not see themselves having a 'permanent' stake in British society, and also to their identification with their Cypriot employers.

Greek-Cypriots and Self-employment

The early employment tendencies of men were to work as waiters and cooks in the catering industry, save hard and set up small businesses of their own. Two examples follow of a move from paid employment to entrepreneurship.

Example 1   Stavros came to Britain in 1948 when he was only 16 from a village near Larnaca. He was brought over by his mother's cousin who had a small restaurant in Kentish Town. His father paid his fare over and when he came to London he lived with his relative and helped in the kitchen and as a waiter. (He is still very grateful for this.) To begin with he saved little as he wanted to have 'a good time', taking girls out (English/Irish) and occasionally gambling. When he was 25 he was introduced by his 'aunt' to a young Greek-Cypriot girl of 18 (Eleni) who was working as a machinist and had also been brought over by an 'aunt' to 'work'. Both Stavros and Eleni migrated for economic reasons and both wanted to remain 'Cypriot' – they had no 'inclination' to become

'Anglicised'. Their relations thought that it was time 'they settled down'. Stavros married Eleni soon afterwards and both worked for 2 – 3 years, living in a small basement flat in his 'aunt's' house and saving very hard. To do this they hardly went out – apart from visiting relatives – and worked overtime. Eventually they were able to buy a small café in North London. Today Stavros owns three restaurants, a large house in Hendon, runs two cars and has built a prestigious house in his home village. He sends every year for his father to come to England and was able to help one of his brothers to come over and study.

Example 2   Andreas today runs 3 dry-cleaning businesses with his brother Petros. They came over in 1961 and started working in small clothing factories as pressers. After a few years they both married Cypriot girls who worked as machinists. They lived in small rented flats, both working for a few years, saving hard and working overtime. When they had children these were sent to a local child-minder. After 8–9 years Andreas had saved enough to open a small clothing factory but this was unsuccessful and he had a series of misfortunes, sinking his small capital into a diversity of ventures. When Petros saved a small amount of capital with the help of his wife the two brothers decided to open a small firm of dry cleaners as they were both experienced pressers.

These two examples indicate the 'natural' progression of employees in clothing and catering towards self-employment. This is facilitated by knowledge and skills acquired in employment, a strong economic orientation, a willingness to work hard sacrificing leisure and life-style comforts, and the employment of women. It is after marriage, usually with the combination of husband and wife's savings that self-employment becomes possible. After it is achieved, it is again more lucrative and successful because of the employment of female relatives. In both cases the wife's labour was responsible for the ability to manage without taking in other employees.

I asked twenty self-employed males how they saved enough to open their small enterprises. Fifteen had combined husband's/wife's saving, ten had borrowed also from kin and seven of them were in partnership originally with brothers or cousins. There is no doubt about the importance of kinship in the self-employment process.

Retail self-employment is a classic avenue of upward social mobility and a 'symbol of opportunity' as Dewy Anderson and Percy Davidson state in a book on 'Occupational Trends in the USA' (1940). They go on to see it as

the age-old field of opportunity by which a person of humble origin
and circumstance may hop to become an owner, secure profits and
achieve a measure of personal security against the hazards of life
(: 450).

Self-employment clearly appeals to the unskilled unemployed and disadvantaged in the labour market but this cannot explain why it is only certain sectors of this population that actually become self-employed.

One important consideration must be the structural conditions that make it both appealing and possible. The over-representation of the 'foreign' born in small business is not a testimony only to their 'drive', but that they possess fewer higher-priced saleable skills in the market place and suffer processes of exclusion. Also the economic motivation for migration spurs them to work long hours in poor conditions for the relative benefits received. However, an additional factor is that they can cater for the special employment and consumer demands of the ethnic group which outsiders cannot meet. As Ivan Light (1972) says on ethnic enterprise in America:

> Since immigrants spoke little English and had their own ethnic culture, they needed stores to supply them with ethnic foods and other services(: 11-12).

However what must be borne in mind is that this consumer-demands theory, as Ivan Light himself points out 'ignores culturally derived differences in economic organisation' (: 18). In Cyprus, economic organisation shows a tendency to 'family' business and there is an entrepreneurial ideology stressing the importance of 'being your own boss' and not being dependent on wage-labour. The notion of 'oikonomiki anexartisia' (economic independence) is an important part of the Greek-Cypriot's evaluation of class position. If they were to stay within wage-labour, Greek-Cypriots would find it increasingly difficult to justify their stay in England, especially given the improved economic circumstances in Cyprus.

Many Greek-Cypriot employers will employ Greek-Cypriot workers and in turn the latter show a tendency to work within Cypriot-owned firms. Greek-Cypriots are able to sponsor and to exploit their own ethnic category through the manipulation of symbols of a known or given commonality of interests between capital and labour. It is true to say that Cypriots to some extent choose to remain within the Cypriot ethnic economy for this may represent the most viable opening economically for them. However, there are additional reasons for this.

Firstly, within the Cypriot small firm they can collaborate with their employers to struggle against a British state that has been constituted as illegitimately attempting to deprive them of their hard-earned wealth and income. The benefits from State provision of education are regarded as important but for many Greek-Cypriots unemployment and pension benefits are regarded as inapplicable. Also many see themselves returning to Cyprus and have no long-term stake in improving social conditions although they may be willing to struggle on local issues. Greek-Cypriots therefore will often prefer to take clear wages without paying tax or national insurance contributions because in their estimation they are 'better off' this way. This is a short-sighted policy for they lose all employment rights, pension rights and the right to unemployment and sickness benefit. In addition they will not be able to claim rent or rate rebates or family income supplement.

Secondly, the Cypriot employer maintains a personal and often familial interest in his employees and there are often social, cultural and political ties between them. This gives a more humanising aspect to work although Cypriots are also strongly aware of the power of the employer in determining wages. Negotiations for wage–rates are at the individual level and many employees do not know the wages given to others performing the same tasks. The male employee however sees his own future economic position within the guise of a small–scale employer and may thus legitimise the mechanisms he himself is subjected to. In addition, Cypriots may prefer to work in a Cypriot firm where they can relate, find work more easily and work hard to further their own self–employment ambitions (as opposed to work which does not provide these advantages). This depiction should not be taken to mean that choice is an expression of the undetermined free will of the actor nor that the class effects Cypriots face are less pronounced. It does recognise however that ethnicity in this case and ethnic segregation at work may be forms of managing migrant disadvantage. Greek–Cypriots who work within the ethnic economy experience opportunities which may be missing for other semi–skilled or skilled workers. (This however is not true for Cypriot women as we shall see in a subsequent chapter.)

An additional factor in explaining Cypriot entrepreneurship is that Cypriot peasant life is highly individualistic and private property in the form of land and housing is common. Cypriots already have a strongly developed ideology of property possession as both a right and a goal. Cypriots migrate to Britain for economic reasons and wish to make use of any openings there are for them. They are willing and able to take risks (either through selling land in Cyprus or borrowing from within the community or using their wives' dowry). Cypriots are also willing to put up with present privations for future rewards and are oriented to some mythical point when they no longer have to. Furthermore, there is little for them to enjoy in Britain – life in Cyprus being life to enjoy. Many Cypriots say they only 'live' when they are on their yearly holiday in Cyprus.

However, of paramount importance is the historical experience of Cypriot migrants and the openings that were available to them in the years of early settlement – openings restricted in a growing economy to those that required neither language or technical skills as in catering. In Clothing too, Cypriots had the important resource of female kinship labour which was the cornerstone of early Cypriot entrepreneurship. The small local shop could also exploit family labour, both of women and children. In the 1960s there were many children over 12 years of age who were an embarrassment to the British educational system which was unable to provide them with special classes. In some schools these children, who could not speak English, were segregated into particular groups and in some cases the school system excluded them completely (personal communication A Zissimos, Islington Cypriot Advisory Centre). Since education was only compulsory in Cyprus until 12 years of age,

Greek–Cypriot parents themselves may have kept such children at home to work.

The geographical concentration of the community, tied to a pre–existing ethnic identification, and to the mode of migration through social networks and patronage facilitated the development of an ethnic economy. This choice of habitat may thus be linked again to the economic and social interests of ethnic groups and allows them to use their ethnic resource both in terms of labour supply and the sale of goods. This in turn served to reinforce the ethnic category, making it unnecessary to go beyond the ethnic group for both employment and services. Thus self–employment was begun from a position of disadvantage but if successful led to distinct material advantages especially in terms of constituting an 'informal economy' not subject to state control. The orientation of the early political organisation of the community to Cyprus, a result partly of the many ramifications of the Cyprus problem, helped to reinforce the ethnic category too. However, the overriding national political orientation of Cypriots is linked to both exclusion processes of the society of residence and the history of ethnic and colonial struggles in the country of origin which were examined in an earlier chapter.

It was not so much the objective unskilled character of the Greek–Cypriot but the type of skills they possessed (skill being an evaluative rather than objective notion) and those they lacked that did not allow them to take on the skilled work some had in Cyprus (Oakley, 1971). The structure of the urban industrial economy makes the practice of small craftswork more problematic and the language problem was often crucial in the type of work taken. The lack of educational qualifications also limited their entry into the labour market to the semi–skilled or unskilled service sector.

Cypriot incorporation into the economy is not dependent directly on racial discrimination but is rather linked to the exclusions faced through lack of requisite cultural capital and limitation of choice in British society. Like other migrants Greek–Cypriots moved into those sectors that had a high demand for unskilled labour (in the case of Cypriots also which did not require language skills). The service sector was the sector where Cypriots were over–represented in relation to their employment in Cyprus. Rapid industrial growth makes new demands on the service sector and the opportunities here were seized. In the case of Cypriots they could expect for example to move into self–employment; often this progress depended on keeping their Cypriotness and using it in a way that was not necessary in Cyprus – that is for economic reasons. The ethnic economy may be regarded as a form of internal sub–colony and it is economically dependent on the larger manufacturing and service sector. For example clothing factories are outdoor units dependent on the large manufacturer. Retail shops too are dependent on larger shipping and import concerns although Cypriots are moving more and more into the import trade.

Cultural disadvantage and not merely racial disadvantage may explain the location of Cypriots in employment. However, Cypriots appear successful through manipulating the system in their own ways in order to escape the bureaucratic management of the industrial sector eg using 'cabbage', ethnic accountants, and paying clear wages to employees.

Racialisation as such cannot explain the original structural location of migrants for we would expect a more similar class distribution for the different categories within the New Commonwealth migrant group as a whole than is actually found. Racial ideology and sectarianism function in excluding groups when they compete with the indigenous population for employment. Although racism is not a product of competition from minorities for jobs, its role as an exclusionary mechanism for employment can only function where there is competition and employers can choose between indigenous and minority workers. In some cases, however, minority workers (as is the case for women also) may be preferred, as they are cheap labour. Visibility is not a static physical property but is related to sensitisation to the different physical, cultural or linguistic groups. Boundaries are constructed dynamically, and ebb and flow according to the socio–economic and political dynamics involved. For example, some Cypriots have a dark skin – as dark as many Asians – but this matter may go relatively unrecognised unless sensitised by structural location and the impingement on indigenous resources.

Cypriot Employment and Migrant Labour Theories

Cypriot employment as we have seen tends to be concentrated in the clothing, service and retail distribution sectors which are characterised by small firms. Immigrants are crucial to the day– to–day survival of these firms for they generally work with low profit margins and are particularly vulnerable to economic fluctuations. They also usually involve poor working conditions, long hours, instability of employment and systems of piece rate. I shall examine the case of female Cypriot labour especially in the context of the Clothing Industry in a subsequent chapter. I argue that the employment of female migrant labour is crucial to the survival of the Clothing Industry.

If we examine the employment of Cypriots in these industries, we find a tendency to work within Cypriot–own firms. This has at least two effects. One is that it serves to maintain the ethnicity and indeed insularity of Cypriots in relation to British society. It also separates them from the political struggles of the working class. In addition it allows for greater exploitation through the higher productivity demanded and lower pay offered by employers often through means of over–time, evasion of tax and non–payment of national health contributions. This latter also has its effects on the State – small capital and the Welfare State being in conflict.

Castells (1975) has argued that migrant labour works in worst conditions, saving in the organisation of work, and has a low interest in participating in current struggles. This is true on both counts for Greek–Cypriots. The ethnicity reinforced by their economic participation serves to isolate them from working–class struggles. Firstly most Greek–Cypriots are not unionised. This is a problem generally for small firms but for Greek–

Cypriot firms in particular. Many Greek-Cypriots do not regard themselves as having a permanent stake in British society. Despite their generally left-wing political affiliations, these find expression in their orientation to the political struggles of the left in Cyprus. The organised left in London fails to take an active stand on internal to the Greek-Cypriot community socio-economic issues such as the relationship between Greek-Cypriot employer and employee.

Cypriots also identify with their Cypriot employers. Their common ethnic and class origin militates against the development of organised class antagonism. Most Cypriot migrants come from a peasant or working-class rural or urban background, finding similar conditions of life and disadvantages in British society on migration. The following factors, amongst others, militate against the development of 'class' antagonism between employer and employee:

(1) A similar ethnic and class background.
(2) The aspiration and movement of employee towards a self-employed status.
(3) Common political, economic and psychological ties with Cyprus.
(4) An orientation to Cyprus for eventual return although in reality this becomes of ideological rather than actual import.
(5) The failure of organised ethnic and political left groups to define Cypriot entrepreneurship as contradictory to the economic advancement of the 'working class'.
(6) The employer is usually a small-scale capitalist often dependent on a large manufacturing class for his survival and on the exploitation of his female kinship and ethnic workers. Thus he is in turn exploited by large-scale capital.

The over-representation of Cypriots in the self-employment category is one indication that the depiction of a generally-formulated notion of migrant labour, as super-exploited, 'sub-proletariat', may be substantively questionable. I have already indicated the economic heterogeneity of the New Commonwealth category as a whole, and indeed that some groups appear over-represented with the 'professional' category. As Westergaard and Reisler note:

> They are certainly handicapped in the labour market, as they are in
> a wide range of other respects, but in no way so as to make them,
> en bloc, an 'under-class' (1975: 356).

Similarly the class differences within the migrant category are often more pronounced than between them and the population as a whole. The class character of migrants at entry accounts in some measure at least, for their occupational distribution in British society. For example, the disproportionate number of professionals from India is related to the growth of migration during the Voucher system period after 1962 where admittance was most usual on the basis of Voucher B (immigrants having required 'skills'). It is as one-sided to consider the constitution of migrants within British society as to see them as possessing disadvantages only structured by their country of origin. It is the interaction between the two aspects that is of significance. To a large extent those writers that note the role of uneven development in the country of origin on the character and process of migration and in addition the processes of exclusion they face within the countries of migration are correct. That however cannot lead us to impute a 'necessary role to migrant labour', nor that migrant labour is a unitary category for the concrete effects will differ (in terms of both the country of origin and country of residence) for different migrant groups and the economic and gender categories within them.

Cypriots have predominantly entered those sectors that require little skill and language ability, where they have acted as replacement workers. As Rex says:

> So far as occupation is concerned, the colonial worker first finds acceptance as a replacement worker. He finds that there are certain jobs... so arduous or unpleasant that they are not acceptable to the majority of the metropolitan working class (1970: 108).

However, in so doing, as Castells (1975) notes, particularly arduous and badly paid jobs are perpetuated − because there are immigrants who do them. For example, in the Clothing sector, deskilling occurs not through the substitution for more capital− intensive labour but perpetuation of cheap labour [see for example Angela Coyle's (1982)]. Certain sectors have possibly survived through the utilisation of migrant labour. The question then arises, how crucial are these sectors for the survival of capitalism itself? As indicated earlier this can only be answered by a concrete study of these and their role within a particular capitalist process.

As Castells (1975) also argues, migrant labour of the first generation enables savings to be made in the social reproduction of the labour force as whole and avoids the costs of rearing the worker. Because migrants often come for a few years on their own without their family it also avoids the cost of family maintenance. Both these elements clearly cannot apply to British born migrants and family/settler migration. This diminishes their economic advantages for European capitalism. A note of caution is needed here, inasmuch as theories of domestic labour have argued the family as a resource rather than a cost for capital.

Despite the problems of developing a 'general theory of migration in late capitalism' presented by the heterogeneity and specificity of its forms we can indicate certain areas where there may exist a common element for migrant groups:

> (a) Migrants work longer hours, are subject to fastest speeds and conditions which may be unacceptable to sections of the indigenous working class, although it is rarely the case that migrants exclusively fill any categories. This is true for Cypriots inasmuch as they work long hours for economic ends and their point of comparison is based either on wages in Cyprus or rates within the Cypriot community. Often the amount of hours they have to work for a given wage is not taken into account. They are often willing to

work for lower wages and thus the returns from them may be higher.

(b) Employers often avoid paying social security contributions since Cypriots have little psychological stake in British society as a whole and may lack knowledge of state benefits. This benefits the employer and the fraction of capital involved. This area could indicate potential conflict between the state and given fractions of capital. Migrants are cheap labour in this sense too.

(c) Migrants may have a limited capacity, on the whole, for 'class' organisation and 'class' struggle within the country of residence, although the ethnic idiom may involve certain class interpolations. For Cypriots this is linked to their employment within small firms which tends against unionisation and their inability to conceptualise their employer as a class enemy through the mediation of ethnic and familial ideologies. Where class consciousness does exist it is often related to class and political developments in a country of origin (as in Cyprus). This may not be true of other groups especially black ones and there are different theorisations of the political/class potential of black groups found in the literature – for example compare Phizacklea and Miles (1980) and S. Hall (1980).

(d) Organisation is difficult because migrants face exclusion on the basis of skills, language, education, culture or racism which limits their real opportunities. These contain struggle since they do not have either the full backing of Trade Unions who are often defensive, economistic and sectarian, nor do they see themselves as sharing the interests of an indigenous working class.

(e) Migrants fragment the working class along the ethnic dimension. Ethnic divisions cut across class divisions and serve to complicate their manifestation. The working class is fragmented already however along sex, skill (socially constructed) and sectoral lines.

Castles and Kosack recognise, like Rex, the wider heterogeneity of migrant workers in Britain than in the rest of Europe but unlike Westergaard and Reisler, maintain that:

> as a whole, it may be concluded that immigrants do form the lowest stratum of the British labour market and that they are likely to continue to do so (1973: 87).

Any analysis which takes into account the sexual category will note that women actually fill even lower positions than migrant groups. In any case, it is difficult to be clear what constitutes the immigrant status. If Castles and Kosack mean those who are experienced geographical dislocation this on its own cannot explain their role in the economy for in Britain there are no distinct legal/political deprivations for those from the New Commonwealth who entered prior to 1962. In which case should we distinguish between migrants who have equal formal political rights and those who do not? In addition, some are Black and other are White and certainly all are culturally distinct. But if 'immigrants' include those whose parents migrated but were born here we have a complex combination of say, Black skin with British nationality and culture. How are these to be located in our theorisation? By Castles and Kosack choosing merely to focus on the economic status of migrants they fail to consider fully the heterogeneity of legal, political and ideological conditions different groups face and their link to economic position. How does one conceptualise, in addition, migrant women who are, on the whole, even lower down the economic scale (as a sub-proletariat?) or the small numbers of indigenous workers who may be found in the lowest-paid jobs or those black or migrant workers who are in well-paid jobs? It is actually difficult to superimpose on class categories, constituted merely through the relationship of a group to means of production, a migrant or ethnic category although one can indicate cross-cuttings.

We are confronted, where Cypriot migrants are concerned in particular, with the problem of migrant entrepreneurship. This is by no means a new problem for Italians, Jews and Greeks amongst others have shown a tendency towards it. The new problem is rather the linkage with colonial migration at a particular concrete period in British society. It clearly serves to problematise theories of migrant labour. (see Anthias 1982 for a full discussion of these theories). However, a number of points may be drawn from this. Whilst capitalist processes may be blind to the non-class differentiations (sex, race, ethnicity), these latter determine the conditions for the sale of labour. Thus capital utilises both sexual and racial differentiation as and when it can and in the process reinforces them.

Capitalism provides, in the abstract, opportunities for all those with capital accumulation (whatever their ethnic, racial or sexual attributes) to extract surplus value from the labour power of their employees. Cypriots are not excluded from this process and in fact have been able to corner a sphere that indigenous capital found too cumbersome in its monopoly capital phase and too labour intensive. Cypriots, among other migrant groups, perpetuate a particular form of capitalist enterprise that was and is shifting increasingly to the colonies themselves, where labour power is cheaper.

The role of migration on the country of origin should also be noted. Remittances, according to Nikolinakos, can have a positive effect, by lessening the balance of payments deficit and thus advancing the interests of the bourgeoisie. However they can contribute also to an increase in the importation of consumer goods from those very countries in which emigrants live and work.

> What they support, in the final analysis, is capital in the immigrant country and the development of policies of the ruling oligarchy of emigrant countries (Nikolinakos, 1975: 12).

Although the advantages of migration are limited, the disadvantages are that it increases the dependency relation between the metropolis and the periphery and deprives the latter of its potential labour and political resources – often it is the young and resourceful who migrate. It can also have lopsided effects on the economic development of the country of origin, as in the case of the investment of migrants in property rather than in industrial enterprises.

This section has considered the special case of Cypriot migrant labour in Britain. Cypriot migrant labour, we have seen, shares certain characteristics which are common to all migrant labour populations. It is mainly replacement labour but functions to perpetuate certain forms of industrial enterprise – in the case of Cypriots, small–scale units. It is permanently resident and the costs of the reproduction are borne by the British state. This means also that they cannot be easily removed when economic developments warrant a contraction in the labour force.

Secondly, migrant labour is a highly differentiated category in Britain. Cypriots, unlike West Indians and more frequently than those from India or Pakistan, show an over–representation amongst the self–employed. They are also more concentrated in retailing, catering and clothing. They are thus usually segregated into small–scale capital concerns. This is not true of West Indians and Asians who are more likely to work for larger factories and firms. Thus migrant labour is not a unitary category. Those theorisations that argue that migrant labour is a reserve army of labour and cheap labour are additionally problematised by the incompatibility of these two notions at the theoretical level (see Anthias, 1980). For if they are constituted as a reserve army they are indeed unemployed and if they are cheap labour then they cannot also function as a reserve for their employment must be preferred for economic reasons. However, in the concrete study of migrant labour there may be political and ideological reasons for disposing of this first even when they may be cheaper – as is the case for female labour. This is substantiated by the greater unemployment of migrants. But this concrete process cannot be understood with reference to a notion of a reserve army of labour – which cannot be used as an explanatory category for differentiated human categories and their employment but should be confined to the position of a 'pool of unemployed' as a necessary constituent of the capitalist accumulation process with definite economic affects for that process (Anthias, 1980). The Reserve Army notion does not take into account job segregation on the basis of sex or race/ethnicity. It may be possible to argue that migrant labour (or colonial displaced populations) can function as a reserve prior to incorporation through their existence as a pool of unemployed and hence as a possible source of employment – this however must be examined specifically with reference to its concrete effects on wages and class consciousness. It may also be argued that migrant populations can subsequently be used as a cheap source of labour but this would entail the use of the indigenous labour force as a reserve. Indeed it is clear that at times of unemployment this is not confined to migrant labour but that women and particular workers within sectors are local labour markets are hit. Where migrants are unemployed this may be due to a variety of factors including:

  a) the economic developments in the labour markets that migrants
  appear in most frequently – either segmented or local markets;

65

b)   for political/ ideological/ organisational factors viz-a-viz employer strategies and working-class sectarianism/unionisation and racism;

c)   because they are not politically organised and lack political representation.

In other words, even where migrant unemployment is greater this cannot be imputed to have its origin in the 'reserve army' function nor does it necessarily have 'reserve army' effects such as lowering of wages and decreasing class consciousness. Any analysis must study the concrete costs and prices of migrant labour populations within the determinate social formation and the economic, political, judicial and ideological conditions under which the sale of migrant labour takes place for different categories within the migrant labour population – including gender and class categories.

Even if migrant labour were constituted as a mere economic category (and in fact most arguments have incorporated within them certain political dimensions and even psychological ones, for example Castells (1975) when he talks about non-identification with the country of residence hampering class affiliation) the problem remains of identifying the 'ethnic group' or 'racial(ised) group' concept (viz Phizacklea and Miles (1980) for example who refer to `Black' migrant labour – meaning Blacks) with 'migrant labour'. For migrant labour refers to a political-legal category, involving an international movement of labour – which in itself cannot be reduced to the constitution of a sub-proletariat or any economic or class sub-grouping. It is the specific economic processes in the countries of origin and the subsequent conditions for the sale of migrant labour in the country of residence that must be considered. In this sense, to attempt to formulate a 'general theory of migration' and 'migrant labour' cannot be undertaken. Nonetheless, certain common features exist in the conditions of the sale of that labour in Britain which constitute it, in a general way, within the lower reaches of the proletariat. It does not from an 'underclass' for it does not have a specific class position of its own.

We shall now turn to looking at various other facets of exclusion, particularly housing, education and ethnic discrimination.

Housing and Class Position

As far as housing is concerned Cypriots were and still are more likely to be living in more densely populated housing, less likely to be in Council housing and on Council lists but more likely to purchase their own houses.

Cypriots share the characteristics of all immigrant groups, despite the variations amongst them, of having larger households, more persons per room, more living in shared dwellings compared to the total population. Despite the affluent life-style many associate with Cypriots, their accommodation on the whole is worse than that of the population as a whole.

In Haringey over half of Cypriots are house-owners, compared to over a third of 'whites' and more than two-thirds of those from the Indian sub-continent who are the most likely to be owner–occupiers. White households are the least likely to be owner–occupiers, but together with 'Cypriots' are the most likely group to own their houses outright. 'Cypriot' and Indian sub–continent households are comparatively unlikely to live in public housing.

The types of houses bought are more likely to be larger ones at the cheaper end of the market; many Cypriots, like other immigrant groups let out a room or rooms and may live themselves in poor accommodation.

Migrants face disadvantages in the housing market. The classical approach is that of Rex and Moore (1967) who develop the notion of 'housing classes' in an urban sociology context. Another conception is that of Dahya (1974) who relates housing more to the cultural choices of migrants. Larger houses allow them to rent out rooms and thus exploit an ethnic housing market. But many migrants live in 'twilight areas' near their work and congregate together to mitigate the alienation and lack of opportunities they suffer in a wider context. Exclusion from Council Housing may be the result of lack of knowledge and inability to manipulate the rules, as well as the residential and time–factor qualifications necessary (Smith, 1974). Exclusion from mortgage–granting facilities may result from lack of knowledge and the requirement of prior investment. Usually, migrants in the early stages of migration will prefer to buy their houses with 'cash' and there is a different conception of home ownership to the indigenous home–owner. Migrants are more likely to let out accommodation in the early stages of migration and themselves live in squalid accommodation. But with their establishment on a more permanent basis they too, like the indigenous population, will prefer to move into the suburbs into smaller family accommodation. The so–called cultural choice of larger housing in inner–city areas has to be considered in the context of work and housing opportunities more generally.

There is great value placed on home–ownership. The opportunity is often limited however to the purchase of properties in areas least attractive to the indigenous population e.g. districts in Haringey with large migrant populations where houses are cheaper. Nonetheless this ownership does provide in one sense a structural advantage that has to be borne in mind in assessing class position. However this is itself related to the exclusion faced from access to other housing and often brought through family help, sacrifice in time, hard work and being willing to put up with sub–standard accommodation initially.

Residential concentration is a significant feature of structural position. In inner city areas, relatively cheap housing which was multi–occupied was available in the early stage of migration as rented accommodation. Other factors are the search for friendship, kinship and solidarity.

Educational Disadvantage

I want to look more closely here at one factor of exclusion which relates to the economic position of Cypriot migrants and its link to their ethnic adaptation – that of education.

A significant element of Greek–Cypriot class structure is the important role of education within it. As a primarily agricultural economy lacking a developed class structure, educational achievement became an aspiration for all social groups in the post–war period with the expansion of state activity in this sector, the growth of urbanism and a tertiary and professional sector. The value of education is attested in the Cyprus Educational Statistics that show that almost 50 per cent of those who finish secondary school go on to higher education. Each parent wants his son to go to college or university (most commonly Greece and the UK) and increasingly desires his daughter to do so. Educational achievement is a dominant value (I do not have the space to explore its implications here in greater depth) and may be regarded as an important element of class and ethnic adaptation. Considering the educational experience of Cypriots in Britain could highlight the importance of education as a means of reproduction of disadvantage and the ghettoisation of migrant worker populations. There may be specific ethnic ways in which class disadvantage is implemented, as Stuart Hall (1978) has pointed out, and if so, what are they? The importance of school and education has been recognised in Marxist theory as having the function of 'skilling' the different sectors of working class selectively – and this is a mechanism for the reproduction of the worker. Paul Willis (1977) has argued that even the 'cultures of resistance' generated are means of transition to subordinate working class sphere. In relation to Black youth, schools have reproduced them at the lower end of employment, production and skill.

The Rampton Report (1981) singled out various factors for underachievement particularly pertaining to the West Indian Child as did the Swann Report and Eggleston Report. Apart from any racism that such children might experience various other factors which may be relevant to the Greek–Cypriot child too have been singled out, although I wish to examine the specificities for the Greek–Cypriot child here. Rampton mentions the inadequacy of pre–school provision, the examination system, teachers' low expectations. It also mentions the loss of trust and lack of understanding between teachers and parents, particularly if the latter are not educated in England. More general points mentioned are the general state of race relations, discrimination in employment, conflict with authority figures and the relative absence of adult models from the ethnic community in prominent positions. It appears that where the ethnic minority is singled out as a problem this can do little good educationally and the teachers tend to have a low expectation of ethnic minority children.

The Swann Report 'Education for All' was published in 1985. It considers various factors associated with underachievement of ethnic minority children, particularly racism, both as ideology and practice and the role of class, region and the educational system itself. It also sets out some of the criticisms that can be made of multicultural education and strongly put the case for the need to challenge racism in the classroom.

Data on Asian children however show such children actually perform better at school despite the wide variety of cultures and linguistic groups they come from. It appears that overall children who were born in this country seem to do better at 16 in reading and maths than those who are immigrants themselves (NCDS study quoted in Mortimore, 1981). The Rampton Committee itself published statistics for six urban local authorities with a high proportion of ethnic minority pupils which was based on the DES school-leavers survey for 1978-9. These data show West Indians perform worse in English and maths than either Asian or Whites.

Evidence however is contradictory and it is not clear what can effectively be said for in most cases socio-economic differences are not taken into account. Craft and Craft (1981) however in a pilot study in London found West Indian pupils performed less well even taking into account such differences. Driver (1980) shows that in terms of public examination attainment West Indian pupils performed better than Whites and the girls particularly so. Asian pupils appear to perform worse at younger ages but often catch up and sometimes overtake white pupils and there is some evidence that Asian and West Indian pupils are more likely to enter some form of further education than other leavers. One explanation relates to different teacher expectations of Asian and West Indian children, the first being defined as more conformist and hard-working. Recent ILEA Literacy Surveys show Asians performing very well.

Regarding Cypriots, the Swann Report got a sense from visiting schools that Cypriot children were underachieving but that Turkish-Cypriots fared worse than Greek-Cypriots. The 1980 Literacy Survey showed in fact that Turkish-Cypriots had the lowest attainment score overall falling behind West Indians. Greek-Cypriots at the age of 8, fell below West Indians as the 2nd lowest scoring group. Swann noted the unintentional racism found in teachers' often negative attitudes to the use of the mother-tongue by the child.

Therefore, although no data have been officially collected for Greek-Cypriot children there is some indication they face distinct disadvantages in particular areas, related as much to the working-class urban context as the racism and ethnicity. During observations in three North London secondary schools I was assured however that Greek-Cypriots had a greater tendency to stay on to sixth form than White pupils and to gain entrance to higher education. For example, in one London secondary school, there were 84 Greek-Cypriot children out of an intake of 1,100. In the sixth form out of 60 sixth-formers, 10 were Greek-Cypriot. The Head thought that about 15 per cent of Greek-Cypriots who enter the school eventually go through to some form of higher education, and thus were well- represented. According to this same Head, the second generation of Greek-Cypriots is not as keen on education as the first generation. Greek-Cypriots tend to be able to find work within the

Cypriot community and thus may not regard higher education as important as did their parents (who value education traditionally as a path to economic and social status).

It appears that those parents with many economic pressures who work long hours expect the school to ensure their children advance. The school in turn interprets this as parental indifference. Those parents who are most involved are the entrepreneurial and more successful. In addition, women deal with children as it is traditionally seen to be the female role but the position of married women as an insecure category in the Cypriot ethnic economy prevents them from taking the requisite measure to foster the child's achievement. As the economic climate has worsened, threatening the small shopkeeper and clothing worker, so children become more disadvantaged. Greek–Cypriot children are fairly well motivated to succeed, but the working class syndrome of low achievement may have already set in as they face similar structural conditions to the urban working class in the more deprived areas of London.

In another school 25 per cent of all children who go to higher education are Greek–Cypriot. This school has an intake of 1,000 pupils overall and a sixth form of 70 – there was a total of about 70 Cypriots in the school in 1980.

Girls and boys according to a third Head performed differently. Girls in particular perform well as long as parents support them and there were 10 Cypriot girls in one school who (out of a sixth form of 100) were studying for 'A' Level. Girls are regarded as more obedient; boys are more likely to be initiated into working–class male culture. It is thus an anomalous situation (as far as gender inequality is generally concerned) where girls tend to do better. This has also been the experience for other minority groups such as Asians and African–Caribbeans. Despite this however, many girls will opt for dress–design, tourism or secretarial work rather than higher education.

Other educational personnel have noted that refugee children brought up in Cyprus (who came over in 1974) have been better performers at school and more motivated than the children born here of long–standing migrants. This is confirmed by my own contacts with children at the Greek–Cypriot classes and discussions with children at the youth–clubs held in the evening.

What must be considered is the relative affect on Greek–Cypriots of a British context on their over–riding motivation for education. We would expect, given data from Cyprus, that approximately 40–50 per cent of pupils would go on to higher education.

Greek–Cypriots came over to England from primarily rural backgrounds having few marketable skills. Since this was the case their initial work was in unskilled service sectors of the economy where, like other economically oriented migrants, they saved greater than the average by living in poor and often squalid accommodation and making do. Their level of education and literacy was poor – in particular for women.

Those families with small children found themselves disadvantaged at school through language. Both knowledge of English and early language

70

development in general were poor because of the extent to which such economic migration involves long hours of work for both men and women, either in the factory or at home. In addition factors relating to different cultural expectations of the school and the school's misconstruction of the child's and parent's own 'class' orientation (in educational terms) are important. For example, the categorisation of `immigrants' as problems at school was facilitated by the tendency of parents to fail to involve themselves adequately in school affairs although less so today, especially amongst the entrepreneurial Cypriots. This non–involvement of Cypriots may be tied to the following factors:–

(1) That in Cyprus, education is left to the teacher, the expert, and parents are not encouraged to participate very much especially after primary level. The schools are closed communities, the teacher is an 'expert'.
(2) The educational system is not often understood by parents nor what the expectations of parents are by teachers. Parents are not adequately communicated with and little effort is often made to involve them.
(3) Many parents who could attend school functions, especially women, do not speak English nor do they have the social skills for a teacher/parent exchange. Men in Cyprus take an active interest in education.
(4) The role of teacher/parent is clear in Cyprus, the social relations set up being part of the status and honour syndrome of Greek–Cypriot society. The father's interest in the education of his children (education being highly valued) is taken to affirm his honour and he does his duty as a good parent. This social relation is missing in Britain, no bonds or community existing between the migrant group and the social milieu of the teacher. This may also function in relation to working–class children within the indigenous population.
(5) The men work long hours and are so driven by economic motivation that they do not find the time to attend schools. Wealth and education are the grounding of class conceptualisation in Cyprus. The Cypriot parent in England still maintains this orientation and wishes the child to excel.

But an additional handicap to the ones already mentioned is that the parent does not know how best to facilitate educational achievement in the British context especially within the predominantly working–class areas that Cypriots inhabit. In Cyprus, the town or village school has a clear social role, each child having instilled into him/her the value of educational qualifications, the community of the school reaffirming and strengthening this, In addition 'what' the parent is required to do is known.

In Britain, the Cypriot child enters a predominantly working class school. She/he is told by parents to study hard, by fellow–pupils that this is makes them a 'boffin', by the teacher that she/he may not be capable, hampered by feelings of cultural difference. The parents do not understand the informal back-up that middle class parents require to guarantee a child's success.

The Swann Report (pages 687–688) cites the following factors as responsible for Cypriot underachievement in schools:

(1) lack of nursery provision;
(2) inadequate English as a second language provision;
(3) inappropriate curriculum;
(4) poor home/school links;
(5) teachers lack of knowledge and understanding of background of Cypriot pupils;
(6) lower teacher expectations and linguistic prejudice;
(7) home/school conflict over cultural values (affecting girls particularly);
(8) a tendency for pupils to 'act up' in freer atmosphere of school compared to home;
(9) influence of both direct and indirect racism.

Despite these problems, there is some indication of a shift towards greater participation of Greek-Cypriots in further and higher education as they become more upwardly mobile, than the population as a whole although we have no means of knowing whether the direction of this involvement is as potentially advancing in class terms. Cypriot participation in higher education shows a preference for economics, accountancy, business, and the professions especially amongst males. Females on the other hand show a preference for arts and with some increasing interest in teaching degrees and sociology. Greek-Cypriot men are instrumental in their attitude to education and a significant proportion may take a degree but nonetheless re-enter family businesses for financial reasons because of the higher economic rewards.

This contrasts with the importance of 'status' and 'esteem' in Cyprus, which is linked to the performance of intellectual and cultural work.

Ethnic Discrimination

Barth (1969) looks at the ethnic category as a boundary marker. However, British society has responded differently at the level of personal relations and ideology to different groups of New Commonwealth immigrants. Afro-Caribbeans have experienced racism, at the level of the stereotype being most likely to be regarded as unclean, immoral, ignorant and beast-like (Jones 1977). The 'Pakistani' (or increasingly Muslim) has been most likely to be seen as insular, poor, ambitious and underhand. Afro-Caribbeans were and are most likely to be picked up by police and were at one time the most conspicuous. Arguably this has shifted to Muslims/Asians, particularly since the Rushdie affair.

In a study on Employment discrimination (PEP, 1967) West Indians were found to face it more regularly than other groups and there are indications that the personal recognition of discrimination tends to be lower than its objective incidence (Smith, 1977 ch.4). A great deal has been written on racial discrimination where Black populations are concerned and I wish to raise the issue of the racism and sectarianism of British society in relation to a so- called White group, the Cypriot.

The early migration patterns of Cypriots did not allow for the development of any clear antagonistic response because of the initial low numbers and fairly inconspicuous character of the migrants. However, as more and more migration occurred from the 1950s and this coincided with the Cyprus struggle for independence, or Cyprus 'troubles' and 'terrorism' (as the British Press chose to refer to it), so more and more Cypriots experienced prejudice and stereotyping. Not only is this a standard response from Greek–Cypriot community leaders but it formed a focus in the activities of Theatre Technis (the Cypriot Theatre Group) in the 1960s. Almost all Cypriots I have spoken to have mentioned this and the problems of finding flats to rent and the prejudice experienced by Greek–Cypriot children at school ('Cyps' or 'Greasy Greeks').

Secondly as more Greek–Cypriots settled and appeared to 'take over' particular inner–city London areas so they became the subject of hostility. The conspicuous consumption of these households that had developed flourishing family businesses, the 'strangeness' of the black adorned 'yiayia', (grandmother) the supposed insularity of the Cypriot, and stereotyping of the Greek–Cypriot male as chauvinist and aggressively sexual are all relevant points. There was special resentment against those who were thought of as 'cowboys' getting 'illegitimate' and disproportionate advantages (illegitimate because they were defined as outside the boundaries of the British national collectivity). In Haringey and Hackney where most of my field–work was conducted, I came across this testament from teachers, council officials, the CRCs and ordinary Cypriots themselves.

Cypriots, like any distinct group faces such sectarianism and chauvinism. It is felt differentially however by those who encounter it in servicing the larger community (in fish and chip shops, Wimpys, etc), where it is often denied, and those who face it as co–workers or co–pupils within working-class communities. Many children attempt to deny their ethnic origin or play it down, do not inform their parents of school open days, are ashamed to be seen out with them, refuse to talk Greek and so on. Children will often admit this – indeed it was true of my own experience as a child – but it was an important focus for discussions jointly run with Hackney Cypriot Association, Hackney CRE and the National Association for Multicultural Education in Summer 1981 and is continually discussed within the Greek–Cypriot community. It is difficult to enumerate the extent to which this is the result of specific acts of discrimination and the extent it is related to the intolerance and sectarianism that characterises much of English ethnic culture. The PEP showed some degree of discrimination against Greek–Cypriots in employment but certainly not as much as for other migrant groups. However, many Greek–Cypriots feel uncomfortable working with English people where they are in small numbers for they are teased about their accents and customs. In schools where there are large numbers of Greek–Cypriot children and other minority children the extent to which it is a stigma is much reduced and similarly with employment (Hackney Cypriot Association etc discussion 1981).

Colonialism in Cyprus did not result in full racial stigmatisation. There were specific conditions in Cyprus for this. Colonialism did not take a properly economic form as it did in the Black colonies for it was motivated by political and strategic aims. Greek–Cypriots were also defined as 'Greek' and as sharing the cultural attributes of the Greek–speaking world that was idealised in British intellectual life. They were also not defined as Black (although many are as dark as some Asians) and historically colour–racism was constructed through the medium of slave society (not merely colonialist relations but the specific form they took in indentured plantation agriculture).

Moreover, Cypriots did not take over or appear to in such a visible way traditional indigenous work (albeit not desired any more). They rather filled vacancies left by earlier minorities, Jews in Clothing and Italians in the Catering Industry. Cypriot women (like other migrant women) took over the jobs that indigenous women had abandoned for the more stable and desirable white–collar service sectors.

This is not to deny however that Cypriots (both Greek and Turkish) are not problematised through their minority status. Language, accent and colouring identify the Cypriot as foreigner. European migration from the developed countries is linked with affluence and status and within the EEC is regarded as legitimate. Cypriots are identified in two ways. Either as poor, low–living ex–colonial subjects or as shrewd, ambitious and resented for 'showing off' their material possessions. Both of these depictions are not figments created to exclude the 'out–group' but rest on real material conditions that acquire particular representation and signification. However, the material effects of these racist stereotypes are not felt as much because many Cypriots have remained within a 'sub' or 'informal' economy and do not compete for jobs with the indigenous population to the same degree as Black migrants. Unlike Black migrants they do not suffer the effects of inter–subjective racism as acutely but rather those of xenophobia, sectarianism and ethnicity.

Inasmuch as racism is one extreme variant of the manifestation of chauvinism and exclusion based on a fixed difference of origin it shares with these a certain form. On the other hand, historically in British society, racism has found both a stronger political and popular expression and is indeed the main form that xenophobia has taken. The visibility of the 'coloured' population signifies their 'origin' difference and acts as a more extensive boundary marker that comes into play and is differentially constructed under particular socio–economic and political conditions. The historical association between colour, colonialism and slavery is of great importance. But racism is not constituted in the same way for all groups. It finds a different political/economic expression towards Afro–Caribbeans and Asians for example which relates to their colonial experience and to their economic role within British society. Racist ideology is not systematic in any sense and contains within it, as Phizacklea and Miles note, (1980) contradictory ideological interpolations.

Racism should not be confined however to the inter-subjective level (as racial prejudice and racial discrimination by human subjects) but takes a more invidious institutional form presented through such diverse elements as administrative procedures and exclusions and the workings of the local state. A central institutional expression of racism is found in the legal system – the redefinition of legal/political status of colonial migrants that has been occurring since 1971, the restrictions on migration from the ex-colonies (with its ideological constituents and effects) that have been occurring since 1962 and the 1981 Nationality Bill. From 1962 immigration laws have been introduced to control entry from the colonies or ex-colonies. Further laws were introduced in 1968 and the Immigration Act of 1971 has extended and sophisticated the process – leading to an effective 'slamming of the door'. While this was occurring white people with ancestral links have retained right of entry and EEC nationals and the Irish have been given privileged rights.

The British Nationality Act 1981 which came into force in January 1983 has restricted the definition of a British Citizen and made it more difficult to acquire such citizenship. Full citizenship was removed from those not defined as 'Patrial' and former British 'Subjects' have had some of their political and civic rights removed. The sexual inequality of these laws is well recognised. These Acts serve to redefine migrant status and could be part of a possible process of repatriation of certain categories who are no longer given automatic right to residence. But legal and political structures have a dual nature. At the same time as restricting the rights of certain immigrants there has occurred a concerted attempt to integrate those who remain and to diffuse possible social problems in a multi-ethnic society.

There has been an increasing interest of the state in 'ethnic minorities' heralded by the growth of agencies catering to their special needs – the 'race relations industry' as it has been called. The growth of the C.R.E. and the local Community Relations Council, the setting up of special advisory and policy-making bodies, the establishment of multi-ethnic education and the introduction (in conformity to an EEC directive) of mother-tongue education within the school system (the whole multiculturalism phase of the race-relations industry) can be seen as reflecting again a dual concern. One is the concern with the social problems faced by minority groups in the sphere of language, social welfare and accommodation to and within the local community; the other is the concern to prevent a problem arising and the recognition of a potentially explosive situation. Also as migrants are concentrated in large urban conurbations, urban policies pay special attention to their situation.

Within the context of the metropolitan cities, migrants are involved in a complex structure of exclusion and incorporation. This is also linked to negotiating mechanisms by the State in relation to migrant groups and the granting of certain concessions. These mechanisms foster divisions along ethnic lines – and struggles may take an ethnic as opposed to a class form. For example, in Haringey, the ability of the Cypriot community to negotiate an expensive 'Cypriot Community Centre' has reinforced the role of the ethnic group as a political mechanism and also structured divisions within the ethnic minorities in Haringey. Some groups have resented this advantage thus conferred to Cypriots who are very strongly organised on a local basis and possess the necessary organisational and political skills.

An additional way of dealing with ethnic exclusion and disadvantage is to use ethnic bonds and familial networks to achieve the economistic aims of migration. Gender relations often become central in this process. This is the subject of the following chapter.

Notes

1   Figures derived from 1971 Census of Population – Country of Birth, Supplementary Tables, Vol II.

5 Gender divisions, the family and ethnic processes

Introduction – Migrant and Ethnic Minority Women in Britain

Women constitute about one quarter of the migrant labour force and over 40 per cent of all migrants (Phizacklea, 1983) but this is an underestimate because of the high levels of unregistered work done by ethnic minority women. Black, migrant and ethnic minority women are concentrated in the most arduous and poorly paid work as well as being subject to the highest levels of unemployment, the exigencies of unregistered work and the deprivations associated with homeworking (Allen and Wolkowitz, 1987).

The commonly held view that women migrants enter only as dependents on their husbands is far from accurate. Like men they came to Britain in their thousands in the post war period until the gates were shut in the early 1970s. Many, both before and after the closing of the gates, have only been recruited on work permits, that is as short term migrants rather than settlers. Between 1963 and 1972 nearly 20 per cent of all Commonwealth workers and almost half of all non–Commonwealth workers who came to Britain on employment vouchers or work permits were women. In the next ten years nearly 30 per cent of those recruited were women, primarily for sectors of the economy where women predominated (WING, 1984, ch.5). Work permits are issued only for jobs where labour supply is scarce. Often it is for jobs that the indigenous work force wont do as in the case of work permits issued to Fillipino women, many of whom additionally come in as 'illegal' immigrants with all that implies (Ardill and Cross, 1987). Black and other ethnic minority women also face racial and gender discrimination which intersects in diverse ways for specific groups of women and in different contexts.

For black, migrant and ethnic minority women, the Anglo morphic ideology of the family and female economic dependency is important. This is despite the fact that for many Afro–Caribbean women at least this is alien to their own reality. For example 31 per cent of West Indian households with children are single parent units (the corresponding figure for white households is 10 per cent and for Asian is 5 per cent (Brown, 1984: 51). This ideology acts to legitimise paying women less than men which has been itself partly structured by men's demand for a 'family wage'

(Barrett and Mackintosh, 1984) and through the notion of the male breadwinner embodied in social security and other Welfare legislation and practice (Land, 1978, Wilson, 1977). They are also confined to low skill (for a feminist critique of the notion of skill see Phillips and Taylor, 1983) and low pay, to homeworking or shift work because of child care, and at times cultural rules. However, they are more likely to be full time than part time workers, unlike other categories of women.

The dominant stereotypes that exist about ethnic minority women see them as passive and subordinate and ignore differences of culture, generation and class (Parmar, 1982). For Asian and Afro-Caribbean women they have a particular resonance, ranging from the victimisation stereotype of the Asian woman (a victim of arranged marriages, strict control etc) to the black female castrator (the strong black woman who cannot keep her man). Such stereotyping not only occurs in the racist discourse of the media but is also articulated within academic work on ethnicity.

One of the most under explored areas has been the way in which gender relations and the family can help us to understand the differential position of different groups in the economy and society (Anthias, 1983). It is not incidental that those groups that have gone into the labour intensive sectors of clothing, catering and retail distribution, particularly as self-employed or small-scale employers, have been those that have used the unpaid labour of women within the family. Cypriot women, for example, have been the cornerstone of the Cypriot ethnic economy in North London (Anthias, 1983) and the same can be said for Asians. The centrality of gender for the understanding of the patterns of settlement of migrant groups has hardly been touched upon in the available literature.

The disadvantages and exclusions that racialised, migrant and ethnic minority women face can be linked to:

a) Their position as migrants –through the legal, political and economic position of migrants but overlaid through the way in which all these processes constitute men and women differently. Here we can particularly point to the position of women in immigration and nationality law.

b) Their position in racialised social relations and the specific form these take for men and women and different groups–here we can point to racism and its effects.

c) Their position as women – and the wide currency of sexism in contemporary societies. This is overlaid by the internal sexist relations of the different cultural practices of the groups. Here we can turn to patriarchal relations and the different forms they take but also to sexist social policy. Ethnic cultural and familial differences will prescribe a distinct set of norms and practices relating to the sexual division of labour–what Kandiyoti (1988) refers to as the patriarchal bargain– and to distinct notions about the different needs and capacities of ethnic minority women as opposed to white women.

d) Their position as members of particular classes but ghettoised into particular areas of employment which are overlaid by exclusions and discriminations on the basis of racism and sexism. This is particularly related to economic positioning.

The issue of the links between gender and ethnic divisions has become an important issue of debate (Anthias, 1983, Anthias and Yuval Davis, 1989). Later in this chapter the links will be examined in the concrete case of Cypriots within the 'ethnic economy'.

A number of general points can be made however regarding the ways in which gender and ethnicity intersect to produce specific effects. It is important not to see the disadvantages constructed by one social division as merely added to by the other divisions as in the triple oppression approach (Westwood, 1984, Phizacklea, 1983).

At the most abstract level, both ethnic and gender divisions construct an 'essence' that can serve to naturalise or legitimise disadvantage, exclusion and inequality. At a more concrete level, gender attributions and sexual and familial arrangements are central elements of ethnic identification and serve to construct the boundary between who can and who can't belong to the group. For example an authentic Cypriot woman or a real 'Kypraia' in Britain conforms to norms of sexual honour and housewifeliness otherwise she becomes an 'Englesa' or as 'good as English'. Further, there is much evidence (Anthias and Yuval Davis, 1989), that national and ethnic groups use women and gender relations to pursue specific ethnic political strategies. For example, women may be urged to have more children as part of a demographic race (Yuval Davis, 1989), they may become symbolic of the purity of the group and promoted as 'mothers of the nation' (Gaitskell an Unterhalter, 1989) or the 'mothers of patriots' (Afshar, 1989). Control of women's sexuality ensures that the ethnic stock is maintained (Anthias, 1989).

National and ethnic processes affect and relate to men and women differently. Their positioning within the state with regard to the law, social services, welfare provisions and citizenship is both different and unequal. Finally, women are central as transmitters and reproducers of ethnic culture as well as being important embodiments of the most 'sacred', and highly esteemed elements of ethnic and national groups.

The rest of this chapter considers gender divisions and the Greek Cypriot family. In particular it examines the extent to which patriarchal relations have been transformed under the different economic and social conditions in Britain. I shall also consider the links between gender and ethnic divisions and the relevance of gender divisions for the continuing salience of the ethnic category for Greek-Cypriots in Britain. In order to examine these issues it is first necessary to look at the traditional family in Cyprus. This both contextualises the discussion and recognises the continuing effectivity of the country of origin for Greek-Cypriots in Britain.

Women in Cyprus

The traditional Cypriot family is rooted in a primarily agricultural economy characterised by peasant holdings. It was not until the 1950s that light manufacturing and industrial production developed to any significant extent and then was organized in small units (Meyer and Vassiliou, 1962).

The Greek Cypriot family can be seen as a variant of a particular Mediterranean family type which itself presents a heterogeneity of nuclear and extended family forms. What has been seen to characterise it however has been the social importance of female sexual purity (du Boulay, 1974). It is nuclear in ideal form but may at times include cohabitation by other members of the family, especially widowed parents. Kinship is bilateral and marriage is forbidden to the fifth degree, ie second cousins may not marry. Marriage tends to be village or town–based various factors being responsible for this including the way in which marriage is arranged by intermediaries which makes local based marriage more likely. Property is transmitted bilaterally amongst offspring and this accounts for the great degree of land fragmentation in Cyprus.

The marriage pattern is one whereby arrangements are entered into by the respective parents and in which the children have the right of veto. In this arrangement discussions concerning the transfer of property to the daughter through the dowry form are made, which for the last forty years or so at least has generally meant the provision by the girl's parents of a house on marriage. Girls with no house find it difficult to marry through 'normal' channels and competition is great for prospective bridegrooms who are able to demand exorbitant claims. I shall return to a consideration of the social importance of the dowry house but now note that this remains legally in the hands of the bride.

Girls are expected to be sexually innocent at marriage and men friends are frowned upon, although increasingly in the towns and amongst the more educated, social gatherings and outings of single men and women are permitted. Men are not expected to be sexually pure and there is an encouragement to find sexual outlets to prove their manhood. This usually means a resort to prostitutes or to the few girls who have a 'low' reputation and are regarded as outcasts, or to foreign girls who come as tourists or to work.

As Peristiany (1966) notes feminine honour is almost always associated with sexual modest. Women until fairly recently could be divorced on discovery that they were not virgins on their marriage night – the old and now largely defunct custom of publicly displaying the bloodied bed sheet is rooted in this.

The arranged marriage involved a buying and selling process – a form of market exchange (Anthias, 1941). The young men and women were both under the patriarchal yoke and were blindly disciplined into accepting their lot obeying the wishes and respecting the 'superior knowledge' of their parents, especially their fathers. This control is illustrated in the case of Georgoulla who came to England at fourteen years to stay with her married brother and when asked for in marriage she sought her older brother's decision as he 'knew better and would want the best for her'. A male brother may act in authority as the father in the latter's absence. The last word in earlier times was allowed the 'Afentis', (the master) as the father was often called. However, the rigid application of this rule is rare in the contemporary Cyprus of the last twenty or so years.

Girls and boys could and can meet at 'panegyria' (the religious feasts), in the fields, in the streets while walking to church or going on the 'peripatous', (the walks) or at the village fountain. The 'sousscs' (swings) strung high in the village centre also provided opportunities for the sexes to espy each other although actual conversation or interaction was rare.

In more contemporary Cyprus, young men and women in the villages may briefly converse at social gatherings, but more informal interaction, in the village street for example, is regarded as undesirable. Although these situations provide certain opportunities for men and women to single out a desirable potential marriage partner, the main consideration always was and still is largely economic.

The ideal partner would have 'a good dowry and good property with good character'. The definition of the latter for the woman combined the element of sexual honour (which if lacking would put into question her domestic or personal worth) and 'prokommeni', that is obedient, domesticated and hard–working. If a woman was 'prokommeni' she was also by definition sexually beyond reproach. Increasingly, however, the more instrumental categories of virginity and dowry are being used, the notion of 'good character' being less salient.

In previous times it was only the parents who went to make the marriage arrangements (proxenia) – that is to make an offer of marriage. The father and mother would go together to the parents of the girl and ask 'Touton to prama ginete' (Is this thing possible?). If there was initial acceptance then the economic details would be discussed – how much money, olive–trees, animals, 'proika' (strictly speaking the household furnishings) and so on would be passed on to the couple by the girl's parents.

If agreement was not immediately possible the bartering would go on until the ship sank or swam – it often sank for a mere fig tree or olive tree.

The enormous importance of the marriage transaction as an economic transaction is clear, as a form of barter and exchange. As soon as the economic transactions were agreed upon a 'fagopoti' (feast – literally eat/drink) would be arranged and the 'loyiasmeni' (the engaged) were usually able to meet under specific social conditions. In the mountain villages where the woman was more likely to be extremely restricted and closed away, the bride kept her distance until the wedding day. But in most cases the couple could meet in her house where increasingly the bride's parents became responsible for feeding the bridegroom, keeping him 'happy' and assuring him of their family honour and their 'means'.

The 'proxenia' are more often done through a third party in recent times. Many villages have their known intermediaries with a reputation for being successful and discreet 'proxenitres' and female relatives are also used. This is a delicate role, for the honour of the family is at stake with a refusal, which often takes the form of 'We are not marrying this year'. The proxenitra is often repaid with continuing friendship, status and presents.

81

In older times, as Loizos (1976) rightly notes, the interval between engagement and marriage could be anything from three to ten years, for marriage required the fulfilment of the 'proikosimfono' (dowry agreement). In some villages and for the poorer peasant there was and still is the custom of the 'hartomenos', (the fiance) moving into the girl's house and establishing sexual relations with her.

The Concept of Honour – Femininity and Masculinity

The concept of honour (filotimo) is a specifically male one, denoting self-respect, masculinity and conformity to the standards of male behaviour. A significant element is to be able to control the behaviour of the women in the family, both wives and daughters, for any transgression by them is an imputation of a failure to exercise proper patriarchal control.

The concept is applied to women however as 'timi' as the possession of honour. For the man on the other hand, it is the orientation or love of honour that is important. For women 'timi' denotes sexual innocence, obedience and domesticity. As Juliet du Boulay (1974) notes, the conception of female sexuality involved the possibility of impurity. Women are the potential victims to their own sexuality which they must be protected from and they are seen as essentially carnal. A woman's loss of honour reflects on the males who control her for they are finally responsible. Men must therefore strive to keep their honour through the control of their family and 'their' women.

The concept of honour operates at the level of conformity to the moral principles of the group and may be tied to class in as much as it works at the level of relations of equivalence structuring intra-class differentiations rather than defining relations between classes (Davis, 1977). A great deal of property bestows status that is not subjected to the honour criteria. According to Schneider (1971) 'honour' concepts are 'cultural codes' and function to construct a unity via the focus on the common familial interests embodied in women in a social system given to possible conflicts over resources (including women as a resource for the reproduction of human labour).

As well as the existence of a double sexual standard, women's sexuality defining the boundaries of family honour, there is a wide-spread feeling that women are 'inferior' and different to men. This is expressed in the old Cypriot dialect by the folk poet Pavlos Liasides (1979: 37).

> As much as they struggle to make the woman like the man, with head great and strong
> It's like those who dress with gold an old tin can, which will scrape off with time,
> The sky always comes out on top – Why?
> Because it's so much higher.

Marriage in Cyprus means for men and women alike the attainment of full adult status. For women, failure to marry involves a total abnegation of sexuality and the continuing dominance of the father. There are no

82

alternative life styles in Cyprus (apart from within small groups of urban intellectuals and artists, primarily in Nicosia) making it difficult for women to struggle against patriarchal nodes of control for they then become social 'outcasts'. Non-marriage is rarely a choice for it involves social marginalisation.

Women in Cyprus are totally responsible for the domestic domain and children, even where they work. The relation between 'honour' and 'masculinity' asserts that it is demeaning for men to do the 'feminine' tasks of child-care, cleaning and washing and if they do they are not exercising proper control. The majority of men believe that they should help in the home only when their wife is too ill or the work too heavy (Markides et al 1978). Women's domestic role extends to services in agriculture add where the male has other paid work is regarded as her sole responsibility. Most women are at their husband's or father's beck and call, often being made to leave the table countless times to bring extra food or drink – the best food is reserved for the men and women generally leave themselves last to be served.

The public performance of conformity to the norm of male dominance is supreme, the wife showing respect and submission although no public expression of affection is made apart from by engaged couples. As with all societies the actual private relations between a man and woman take a wide variety of forms, however, although there are certain limits beyond which a woman cannot go such as outright rudeness to her husband. It is the social control exercised by the ideology of male dominance and its public expression that is significant.

Writers have often referred to the Greek concept of shame (tropi) as denoting public dishonour as opposed to the notion of guilt which denotes an internalised feeling of transgressing moral rules. According to Adamantia Pollis (1966) this latter requires a particular notion of the human subject/individual that is not found within the Greek-speaking world. In Cyprus it is what you 'do' and its social interpretation that matters, for what you 'are' is always defined with reference to this.

Although the norm of public submissiveness to the male is dominant certain deviations are allowed especially where a woman has been forced to marry a man who is 'beneath her' or where she is totally economically independent from him. There is a recognition therefore that masculine 'honour' is related to the proper performance of the economic role of chief 'provider' and there is a certain fear of a woman who earns more than her husband.

Marriage in Cyprus must lead quickly to motherhood. In a study of Lysi village (Markides et al 1978) in the Famagusta region the majority of first births' arrived a year after marriage to prove male virility and fulfil women's 'natural' maternal role. Parents expect sons to gain a 'good' education, to be assertive, (although submissive to the father – smoking in front of him or attending the same coffee-shop being frowned on) and to indulge in sexual relations as and when they can.

Daughters are expected to be obedient, domesticated and modest and increasingly to gain a 'good' education also, for this improves their marriage chances and not primarily because it is valued in its own right for furthering the girls' occupational choice, although parents are proud of a doctor or lawyer daughter. Nonetheless, even here marriage is the ultimate goal for women.

There are rarely friendships across sexual divisions for workers or peasants, for these are always associated with sexuality. Women are conceived as always on the brink of being 'fallen wantons'. Class differences exist however and amongst the urban bourgeoisie such sexual 'contamination' is not always imputed and so friendships between the sexes are more permissable.

The Dowry House

What is clear in any discussion of the Greek–Cypriot family is the supreme authority of the father. Indeed, even a married woman's final submission is to her father and through him to her family of descent, rather than to her husband. This finds expression in the 'dowry' form, which in contemporary Cyprus, as already noted, involves the transference of a house to the woman on marriage. According to Loizos (1976) the universal application of the rule is primarily a result of demographic factors in Cyprus since the 1930s when women (partly through the migration of men but also other factors) existed in greater numbers than men in the favoured marriage age–groups.

Prior to about 1930, according to Surridge (1930), the

> bridegroom provides lands, animals and a house, except in certain hill villages in Paphos and Limassol, five near Morphou and the villages close to Nicosia where it is provided by the bride.The bride provides lands, furniture, cooking pots, bedding and personal clothing (: 25).

It appears then that the custom here was local and even villages side by side (like Kontea and Lysi in the Famagusta region) had different customs. Until 1974 in Lysi men still on the whole expected to build the house on marriage (Markides et al, 1978). It is not clear however why demographic balance, making men scarcer, should result in the house–dowry form. Ifeka's (1977) counter argument is that it must be considered as part of a patriarchal strategy of control but this clearly requires more specification. For the house transferred on marriage is legally to the bride and remains her property. Control is finally in the hands of the father (often using property gained from his wife's dowry) who can not only continue to control his daughter through this means but also his son–in–law who is forever in his debt. Where conflict between father and husband occurs in these cases, loyalty to the patriarch ad his family lineage is assured. Father however loses control over his own sons who become his potential competitors. What unites them however is their vested interest in the control of daughter and sister. Brothers may avenge their sisters dishonour end must wait their turn to marry after she has settled down.

The implications of the dowry house are many. It reaffirms family and kinship networks and the economic obligation of the woman to her father. It leads to families remaining close to one another for the land the house is built on is usually in the same village and often the same street as the parents. Sisters will tend to live near each other facilitating even more parental control. However, the dowry house has implications that are contradictory,for it provides a certain amount of economic independence for women. The husband may be legally thrown out and become homeless although other ideological and social forces generally prohibit this. The full implications of this legal property possession still remain to be explored however. What is undoubted is that parental power over women resides in property control.

Loizos' main thesis is problematised in two ways. Firstly the house has not changed sides as he appears to assume for there were always different tendencies in different villages that need to be accounted for. If we can account for these we may arrive nearer to an adequate explanation. Secondly even if this had occurred it does not necessarily mean a shift in power between the sexes over marriage choice, nor that men have to be offered more enticements in the form of the house. For it may be that women have always made a greater economic contribution to the setting up of the household. Loizos' argument is ahistorical and does not take into account the total system of social relations within which any shift has occurred. For one thing, houses prior to the 1940s at least, were mud houses, built by the family themselves – the bridegroom would build his own house and the cost was not exorbitant. The bride on the other had provided furnishings, land and other goods which in money terms may have meant a greater outlay. Even where the bridegroom built on his own land, land values were low before the 1940s, a houseplot being worth only a few pounds.

Any explanation of a shift in dowry customs must take into account a) changes in land values and b) building materials, customs and technical standards, which make house building more of a skill requiring architects, designers and skilled workmen.

What is clear is the extent to which the dowry house is a condition for defining the position of women, denying her personal human value, transforming her into a strictly marketable commodity, reducing her freedom to choose and making her right to sexuality (only possible through marriage in Cyprus) dependent on the economic position of her parents and their ability to provide her with a house.

The extent to which this dehumanises women ad constrains them is indicated by the following case:

> Androulla is one of three daughters and she is twenty-three years old, fast approaching an age when she must marry soon to remain eligible. In addition until she marries her two youngest sisters must also wait. Androulla fell in love and had a non-sexual but public association with a co-villager who did not wish to marry her. This makes her chances on the marriage market worse. After several

years of looking for a potential husband her parents have found Andreas, who has high stakes as he is a University graduate. He, however, has demanded a two-storey house in the town (where land is expensive). Since her parents only have land in the village this places great strain on them. However they were able to buy a plot in the town and the engagement party was arranged. On the night he failed to turn up and after some enquiries it was found that he had further demands, including a new car and expensive furniture. They have no choice but to concede and she is continuously on tenterhooks that he will withdraw, demanding more.

The case of Eleni also indicates the social cost of the dowry for women. She was unable to provide any land or property as her father died unexpectedly leaving a great deal of debt. She failed to marry although she was both attractive and a good housekeeper (both attributes that are valued in Cyprus) and given the social relations Cyprus remained dependent on her parents and has never reached 'personal fulfilment' which in Cyprus is defined through the achievement of a 'good' marriage.

Women's Economic Participation and Sexual Divisions in Cyprus

Women in Cyprus have always been involved in production for in the traditional peasant agriculture–based economy women's and to a lesser extent children's labour was essential to the subsistence of the family unit. They not only worked alongside their husbands in the fields, but as Surridge (1930) notes:

if the holding is insufficient to maintain the family, work as agricultural labourers or on the roads (: 26).

In addition women weaved cloth on primitive looms and in certain areas, such as Larnaca, Limassol and Nicosia they made lace which they sold, many through selling outlets in Lefkara. Surridge (1930) says:

lace–making is injurious to the eyes and to the more delicate parts of a woman's frame owing to the posture adopted. Childbirth is often difficult on this account (: 26).

The heavy agricultural work women did made them old and worn and they continued working until labour and delivery. Children too were involved in production often working for other families, long hours from 'sunrise to half an hour before sunset' with a two hour break. Many girls in addition worked as domestic servants or 'Kores' (literally virgins) and Surridge estimated about 20 per cent of houses in town employed them often as young as eight years of age. They were often brought up by their employer and expected to work long hours, doing heavy work. Some girls were provided with dowries but other girls were ill–treated or sexually abused.

In addition to work in the fields women were responsible for tending the animals, collecting the yield from carob ad olive trees, producing olive–oil, fetching water from the well or village fountain, making halloumi (a cheese made from goat's or sheep's milk), grinding corn and wheat into flour and pourgouri (cracked wheat) making 'trahanas' (soup from wheat ad yoghurt) and drying it, making the family's clothes, as well as cooking, cleaning, tending the children and all the other tasks of domestic labour. Much of this employment was hidden in the household for it did not reap a wage and merged into domestic production yielding use values. Halloumi, cloth, trahanas, olive-oil and other produce was also often for exchange.

Peasants in Cyprus under both Ottoman Rule (1571–1878) and British Colonial domination (1878–1960) were subjected to a peasant/merchant intermediary system which provided selling outlets for agricultural produce and as late as the 1940s and even 50s, was an important but debilitating source of credit. (Attalides, 1977). Debts were rife in Cyprus and the dowry system contributed to this – Surridge estimated that 60 per cent of dowries were paid from loans (Surridge, 1930). Interest rates were both arbitrary and exorbitant and land and property often had to be auctioned off at the 'Demoprasia' (public auction) to repay them. Many of these conditions still existed up to the 1950s although urbanisation and the growth of light manufacturing and the construction industry were on the ascent (Meyer and Vassiliou, 1962).

Sexual divisions in Cyprus were and still are characterised by the dominance of patriarchal relations. However there are various processes that have occurred since the 1960s that indicate a transformation of some of the elements discussed. One of these is a general loosening of the strict norm of sexual purity especially in the towns and amongst the most modernised sections in the villages. Class differences have always existed in sexual behaviour but these tended to be between a small urban bourgeoisie and the mass of the population. Increasingly the tertiary and middle sectors are moving towards allowing some degree of sexual freedom to girls, including allowing them to go out in groups with boys and to have friends of both sexes. However it is still difficult for a girl who is known not to be a virgin to marry without a larger dowry as a recompense. Thus the external manifestation of freedom around sexuality is greater than the real shift.

Secondly, women in Cyprus are increasingly participating in secondary and higher education. Since the latter by necessity has to be abroad, it often acts as a break in the patriarchal control of the father and provides opportunities for alternative, more sexually free, lifestyles and concomitantly the development of oppositional feminist ideologies.

Thirdly, as more and more Greek–Cypriot women become active in the labour market, so some aspects of patriarchal control will be modified, although any great transformation of sexual relations to accompany economic participation has yet to be seen.

I shall now turn to a consideration of Greek–Cypriot women in Britain.

The patriarchal nature of the Greek−Cypriot family has already been testified to. To what extent is this transformed within the British context? In order to tackle this issue,it is necessary to examine its adaptation to the social and economic conditions in which migrants to Britain found themselves.

Greek Cypriots emigrate for primarily economic reasons and to provide better opportunities for their children. Given the economic aspirations and the desire to accumulate a nest−egg for eventual return to Cyprus, it became a necessity for women to work too. It was however unthinkable for women brought up in the enclosed world of traditional Cypriot rural life (the majority of migrants being of rural origin) to enter into unskilled manual work in foreign and 'dangerous' male−regulated jobs. There was the additional factor of language and lack of self−confidence since most women had only worked at home or in the fields. The Cyprus economy was mainly agriculturally based until the 1960s by which time most emigration had been completed.

When men sent over for their wives and families they had often worked in Britain for a year or more, as waiters, shoe−makers or tailors and some had accumulated a small amount of capital. Their aspirations were to have their own small family business which was partly related to their earlier role as peasant producers. In addition, rents for cafes and small restaurants were cheap in the central areas of north London that they moved into. The earlier establishment of a caucus of Greek−Cypriot migrants was a relevant factor here. These small Greek−Cypriot owned cafes employed their womenfolk and were only viable given their employment.

The earliest clothing factories were small family concerns often two or three brothers or relations setting up a small business on limited capital, filling the openings left by the declining clothing manufacturing sector (the East− and West−End 'sweat shops', Shah, 1975). The boom period of the British economy in the 1950s and 60s had increased worker expectations and aspirations and the conditions, pay and instability of this sector of the labour market left openings for migrant labour. In addition women brought the traditional sewing and cooking skills with them which could be exploited in this setting.

Cypriot female migrant labour provided a pool of often unpaid or at least cheap labour involving the direct extension of production for use into production for exchange and of the patriarchal relations of the family into wage−labour. This subservence of the female within her economic role to her husband, brother or father helps us to understand in part the way in which the incorporation of women into economic production failed to transform sexual divisions. That is not to deny that women gained certain advantages and freedoms. Where women worked, they could contribute to providing a home, regarding it as joint property. Even though in the sphere of sexual roles, this had little effect, nonetheless it provided women with more clout as far as sexual negotiations were concerned. For example, an issue that many was were forced to confront when they initially came over was their husbands pursuit of women who were willing to enter into sexual relations without the need for life–long commitment. Some men had even established long–term on–going relations with another woman. Cypriot women were more able to refuse to countenance such situations given their economic contribution.

Another offshoot of women's economic contribution was to increase the 'cash–nexus' of the Cypriot woman. A significant characteristic of the Cypriot migrant is that economic success is sought as an attempt to improve his status within the class system in Cyprus and within the fairly self–contained Greek–Cypriot community in London. The woman, who if she does not work, often argues that her home and children are more important than money, now wishes to accumulate more, often insisting that this is her money rather than ours (this may be linked to women's legal possession of property in Cyprus via the house–dowry form).

Economic motivation may begin as a necessity of subsistence but may also involve a competitive and consumption oriented social display. The Greek–Cypriot life–style in London is directed to the Greek–Cypriot community in Cyprus and London and emphasises conspicuous consumption – property ownership, large car ownership, big spending and lavish furnishings. The main difference between the 'Barnet' and the 'Haringey' Greek–Cypriot is that the first is more economically successful and more likely to own his own business than the second. Cultural and other attendant characteristics of 'class' position are often missing.

Certain suburbs of London are designated as status areas, like Hendon, Finchley and Barnet. Those who live in Hackney are more likely to live in Council Houses, those in the suburbs,in 1930s semi detached villas. It is women's exploited but often lucrative work that contributes to the social move from one area to a 'better' one.

Greek–Cypriot men still expect their wives to be solely responsible for child–care and domestic labour even when they work full–time, over–time and receive reasonable wages. She may return home exhausted, tend her children and her husband, do her housework and shopping and then collapse into bed. It is not surprising then that women are some of the most dissatisfied members of the community and suffer from ailments and depressions so frequently (Cypriot Women's Health Group, Haringey). Men on the other hand when they finish work (although they too work long hours, and if they have a small business in the evenings and weekends) can retreat to the cafeneion society or clubs that are a masculine domain, such as exist in the Finsbury Park area of Haringey. They go there to retreat from their family and rediscover the male life–style of their home–land. Older women may serve in these cafes for they can no longer stand as sexual beings. Nor do women enter these cafes to accompany their men.

Despite the dissatisfaction of Cypriot women they rarely see any other alternatives open for them. For example in a study conducted by the Haringey Area Management Team, Greek–Cypriot women had a much lower than average desire to 'retrain' (West Green Child Care Survey

Report, 1981). The definition they have of themselves is as wives and mothers first.

Women's sexuality has remained largely unchanged within the British setting, parents stressing the need for virginity and frowning upon boyfriends. There exists a tension therefore between traditional Greek–Cypriot sexual mores and behaviour and those of British society and this often expresses itself in the relations between parents and their daughters. However, girls and women cannot be so closely supervised as in the villages in Cyprus. This is especially the case for younger women who are more likely to work as secretaries or clerical workers in non–Cypriot establishments. Parents are more concerned about the public display of sexual behaviour and thus 'what will they think of us' and tend not to be so pristinely traditionalist in the larger and more anonymous environment of London or the other large cities in which Cypriots have settled, although more so than in urban contemporary Cyprus. Also girls and women are subjected to a set of different norms and practices in relation to female sexuality and will have been introduced to debates concerning women's rights, equality, sexuality and feminism.

To some degree girls manage the dissonance between wider societal and parental values and expectations. Most Cypriot girls do not openly flout their parents expectations, but are more likely in private, to entertain different attitudes. Some Greek–Cypriot girls have boyfriends and may have full sexual relations with them. Parents may be uneasy about this but are willing to accept it as long as public display has not taken place and as long as parents are assured in their own minds that the girl is still a virgin. Although parental attitudes vary there has been some easing of the material expression of the ideology of sexual purity. In addition the material reality of the oppression by the dowry–house has largely disappeared. A common practice is that parents will provide financial help with setting up home. Those who can afford to may transfer land or property in Cyprus. But this is an added bonus for the bride and groom and not mandatory. Marriage is no longer a clear economic transaction although often economic considerations weigh into the choice of marriage partner for both men and women.

Women also have the opportunity to marry a non–Cypriot which some do, preferring Englishmen to members of other minority groups. Greek–Cypriot girls and boys would prefer to marry another Greek–Cypriot and most in theory maintain the notion of female 'honour'. However, material circumstances as they become older may transform the actual expression of these notions. Many Cypriot girls will revert to a more Cypriot environment once they leave school and increasingly devoting their leisure to social activities within the Cypriot community. Girls are often provided with cars, clothes and have been brought up to submit to parental will. A further factor in this is that the geographical, social, economic and political links of the Greek–Cypriot community act as effective policing mechanisms. Greek–Cypriots congregate in particular areas, many of them working there and having a close network of family and relatives. Under such conditions, traditional sexual relations and roles are preserved.

Many Greek–Cypriot girls are discouraged or forbidden from 'going out' with non–Cypriot girl–friends. Many Greek–Cypriots have a low view of English women, regarding them as sexually promiscuous and they do not wish their daughters to associate with them.

Older Cypriot women in London are still subordinated to men. Despite the reasonable pay many women receive as machinists in clothing factories, they have little security or power in their work, their hours of work or conditions. In addition separated or divorced women may be subject to gossip in the social setting of the Cypriot dress factory where most needs work, given the dominance of marriage and the family in Cypriot society. There are limited opportunities or alternative life–styles available for such women within the Cypriot idiom in London, since they often barely speak English and/or have no social contacts with English people. Their friends are likely to be family friends for Greek–Cypriot women of the older generation rarely have purely personal friendships.

Women are not totally absent from the ethnic organisational scene and indeed are mainly responsible for transmitting Cypriot culture through their participation in the youth–clubs and activities that often take place after the Greek language schools in the evening and on Saturdays. They teach dancing, singing, folk–lore and tradition. Women have also been represented in all ethnic organizations, including educational and political ones, such as the Greek Parents Association which is a powerful educational organisation. Many of these women, like the men are 'progressive' women whose political background is found in the 'progressive' political, syndicalist or women's movements in Cyprus. Their husbands too tend to be involved actively in ethnic organisations. It is rarely the case that women whose husbands have been isolationist organisationally have been able to make the break–through both psychologically and socially to participate.

It is difficult to estimate the extent of participation but it is often the same small group of women who are highly active in

(a)   cultural events – organizing youth–clubs and dancing classes;
(b)   the Greek–Cypriot Women's Association – an ever present but only sporadically active group some of whose main organisers are long–standing ethnic/political activists in Britain for 20 to 30 years;
(c)   the Parents Associations and the schools.

Sexual Divisions and the Ethnic Boundary

Women are carriers of ethnicity in two senses. Firstly they were the building stones of Cypriot entrepreneurship. It was the exploitation of female kinship labour that was the first form that this took, later to be supplanted or supplemented by 'gnostous' (acquaintances) and mere employees, most of them Cypriot. This involved the extension of patriarchal relations into wage labour relations. Secondly, women are the direct transmitters of the 'cultural stuff' of ethnicity but not only because of their dominant day–to–day role in domestic and familial life and in child–rearing. As in many societies, women are the direct controllers of

91

female sexuality. For Cypriots in London, it is the woman who 'polices' her daughter, who represents a model of chaste sexuality and who teaches taboos about menstruation, for example. One taboo is that women must not enter a Church or kiss the ikons if they are menstruating as this is seen an act of sacrilege. Menstruation is contaminating and expresses female sexuality (which is dangerous and powerful – women conceived as always ready to fall prey to it). Women must not have sexual intercourse when menstruating as this is believed to result in having a deformed child. Women should also not bathe during menstruation as this endangers their health. Nor must they exercise. There exist taboos about contraception too and many women are taught by their mothers that their use will mean the possibility of barrenness.

Although women are the transmitters of the 'cultural stuff' of ethnicity they do this as mediators between the patriarch and his children. Women who do not perform their obligations as cultural transmitters of ethnic ideologies are failing to preserve the 'honour' of the male. A woman often acts as mediator between her children and her husband, communication between them being through her and she acts as a sieve and censor of its contents. She often makes rules in the idiom 'your father doesn't like it'. The sexual values she purveys are those grounded in a male–dominated society that sees women as a resource and wishes to guarantee father–right and ancestry. The taboos on women's sexuality, shame of the body and sexual feelings are constructed via the mother but in conformity to the requirements of a male–dominated society.

Ethnicity, however, is neither the 'cultural stuff' nor the life–style of the ethnic group although these are implicated within it. Ethnicity is the denoting of the 'ethnic' as a significant arena for struggle. Ethnicity is a modality for pursuing the aims of the group. These may be class, political or indeed sexual political aims. In the earlier discussion ethnicity expressed sexual political aims. The following case is an example of the supreme authority of the father:

> Aphrodite fell in love with a young Greek–Cypriot and wished to marry him. Her parents regarded him as unsuitable for they had aspirations for her (as many Cypriot parents) that she should marry someone with education, 'good' parentage or money. She insisted and threatened to live with him. Her father disowned her against the expressed wishes of his wife who was forced to concede under verbal and physical threats. The wife was not only intimidated however but she felt that obedience to her husband was more important than her own wishes and her desire to love and support her daughter. Aphrodite lived with the man until she was able to marry him legally without her father's consent. Neither parent had any contact with the daughter for seven years even though she lived close by. The mother knew her situation as they had a mutual acquaintance. The daughter had two children but still neither parent relented although the mother desperately wanted reconciliation.

This story has a happy ending as a male relative from Australia came over and took it into his hands to patch the relationship up. It is significant that this was only possible for a man who could not impute 'dishonour' to the father as he was a wealthy and respected relative outside the community.

Women transmit the values of 'good' Greek–Cypriots or 'patriots', those of sexuality, the 'work–ethic' and nationalist consciousness. A similar argument is made by Alan Hunt (1981) in relation to the role of women for the 'New Right' in America. The Mother–Nation twin is important here as is the notion of 'Mother' of 'Fighting Men'(see Anthias and Yuval Davis, 1989).

Women are also definers of the ethnic boundary. This works both in terms of the legal definition of citizenship; only particular women can reproduce citizens within the 'national boundary'. For example in Britain the Nationality Bill which came into force in 1983, constitutes those women who are defined within the new national boundary as having an 'independent right to transmit to their children British nationality' (WING, 1984). At the same time it excludes particular categories of women who reside in Britain from reproducing the national collectivity. However another aspect of ethnic boundary definition is entailed by a whole system of sexual relations concerning who can marry whom which relates more rigidly to women than to men. This works both in relation to control by the dominant group and also in relation to processes of reproduction of the migrant group through restrictions on the marriage of say Cypriot women to non–Cypriot men. The attempt to maintain ethnic reproduction can be linked to patriarchal control so that children of such women are not lost to the ethnic group. The ideals of purity and sexuality are linked to the very definition of a good ethnic subject defining for example a significant boundary from those who were born into but no longer stand effectively as ethnic subjects. For women this entails behaving in ethnically appropriate ways by conforming to the principle of sexual purity and for men entails maintaining control over women. 'En telia Kypraios' (he's a true Cypriot) means he is patriarchal and controls his women effectively.

Women are generally more active in the religious and cultural relations of the ethnic group and these tend to involve sexually distinct modes of behaviour. Indeed where migrant groups are concerned, when men come over on their own, ethnic culture tends to greater decline (Dench, 1975). Ethnicity intersects with gender divisions and the patriarchal family unit.

Women are the bearers, keepers and symbolic signifiers of ethnic identity and constitute one of the most important boundary–markers between English and Cypriot ethnicity. The patriarchal character of the Cypriot family constitutes an important element in explaining the economic adaptation of the Greek–Cypriot migrant, providing a pool of cheap available labour for small–scale entrepreneurial concerns.

Cypriot women in London are still subjected to sexual norms and practices pertaining to an earlier period in Cyprus, one which has been transformed in Cyprus itself in terms of sexuality if not of patriarchal control. However the material conditions in Britain – the greater social and economic freedom of women and the availability of alternative codes of behaviour means that objectively women experience greater opportunities for freedom.

In the following chapter, the focus will be on the links between gender, ethnicity and class through an examination of Cypriot women and work.

Their greater economic independence is a significant element here and their non reliance on the dowry system for marriage. In the following section, I shall look more closely at the economic position of Greek Cypriot women in Britain and their role in the ethnic/economic adaptation of Greek–Cypriots to British society.

6 Women's work: Ethnicity and class

Ethnic Minority Women and Work

I shall now turn to a more detailed discussion of ethnic minority women in the labour market for this provides us particularly with an obvious arena for examining the links between gender, ethnicity/race and class.

The intersection of sex and race in employment has to be understood empirically in the context of the internationalisation of the labour market and the tendencies of firms to move to the periphery to draw on the cheap labour of women both in the third world and in the advanced societies. This has occurred side by side with the creation of two labour markets, one for permanent white men (a core) and an impermanent casual predominantly female one which includes part time work (Mitter, 1984). The ethnic minority population on the whole has filled jobs that the indigenous population did not want and it is these jobs, labour intensive in what can be called the underdeveloped sectors that have been most at risk in the recession. In this light ethnic minority women particularly have faced long term unemployment and unlike the men have not moved more into self-employment or the hidden economy – where they have it is to assist their men as unpaid family workers.

National data on employment suffers from the handicap of using highly heterogenous categories – for example, the term 'black' workers may be used and at times it is not clear which groups are included in this category. There is also the danger of treating the categories as homogenous given that the groups within the shifting 'black' category have diverse employment characteristics. But an additional difficulty is found in terms of the way in which the collection of data often hides rather than illuminates both the real differences between men and women (Oakley et al, 1971) and the differences between white women and ethnic minority women.

In terms of economic activity Brown's survey (Black and White Britain, 1984) shows that West Indian women have particularly high economic activity rates (74 per cent) compared to white women (46 per cent) and Asian women 39 per cent (Muslim women 18 per cent, Hindu women 59 per cent, Sikh women 54 per cent). West Indian women are more likely to work full-time than other women – the 1981 Labour Force Survey found 42 per cent of West Indian women compared to 23 per cent of white women and 25 per cent of Asian women were in full-time employment. Also West Indian women have average weekly earnings that are about £4 higher than white women and £8 higher than Asian women (Brown, 1984: 212). Different categories of ethnic minority women occupy different parts of the labour market with Asian women over-represented in the textile and clothing industries, in repetitive assembly-line work and as homeworkers, and West Indian women more likely to be in low grade professional work and in the service industries (Brown, 1984: 203).

In relation to unemployment, in 1984 19 per cent of ethnic minority women were unemployed compared to 10 per cent of white women workers with Pakistani and Bangladeshi women having the highest rate – 40 per cent, followed by Indian women – 18 per cent, and West Indian women – 17 per cent. This is likely to be an underestimate as it refers to registered unemployment.

We have to treat published data with some caution, however. Empirical studies of racial disadvantage (eg D Smith 'The Facts of Racial Disadvantage' 1977, and C Brown 'White and Black Britain PSI, 1984) have often claimed that differences in occupational levels, pay and employment are not as great between black and white women as they are between white and black men – the disparities are lower because sexism already disadvantages women in the labour market to such an extent that the effects of race are not so apparent. This is a gross over-simplification for a number of reasons.

Various studies, particularly of home-working (eg Allen and Wolkowitz, 1988; Hoel, Anthias, 1983; Mitter, 1986) show that many ethnic minority women are not part of the registered working population. This implies that the economic activity rates in published sources underestimate the extent of women's participation in the labour force and may not give a full picture of its nature. For example, women from ethnic minorities have a greater tendency to work in small scale factories, retail shops and restaurants (apart from Afro-Caribbean women) and as unpaid family labourers (eg alongside their husbands and other members of the family). This indicates that the real average wage levels may be much lower than official statistics show. Similarly if we take shift work and number of hours worked into account then the actual wage rates are lower than they would appear otherwise. This is because the number of hours worked and whether they are done in unsocial hours (shift hours) is not represented in the data on wage levels and we know that ethnic minority women work longer and more unsocial hours than other women. Also, because ethnic minority women (like men) tend to be concentrated in the South East where wage levels tend to be higher anyway, then the picture of average national wages and employment levels gives a distorted comparison. Ethnic minority women are more likely to work full-time than white women and their younger age distribution compared to whites also has to be taken into account in interpreting the data available (for a useful account see Bruegel).

There is also the problem of job classification. Women are bunched in non-manual work in official statistics but this conceals the nature of these non-manual jobs and the over-representation of women in the lower echelons of technical and clerical work in the tertiary sector of the economy (see Oakley et al, 1971). Regarding ethnic minority women, they may fall into the same broad categories as white women but this may hide the fact that they are more likely to be in lower status and paid work within these categories as is the case also for ethnic minority men). Despite these problems it is clear that ethnic minority women have a tendency to both high economic activity rates and to be in full-time employ in different sectors for different categories with Asian and Cypriot women being more likely to work as family or home workers than West Indian women.

Full-time and high economic activity rate may be accounted for in a number of ways. One of these relates to the generally lower employment status and pay of ethnic minority men (see Cook and Watt, 'Racism Women and Poverty', in Glendinning C and Millar J (eds) 'Women and Poverty in Britain', Wheatsheaf, Brighton, 1987). There also exist cultural differences about women's capacities and roles vis-a-vis the balance between the sexual division of work in the home and in paid work, different familial structures and expectations and for First generation migrants the economistic aims of migration including for some group[s, dependents in the country of origin and the 'myth of return' (see Dahya, 1974; Anthias, forthcoming). However, a detailed analysis of some of the processes that can account for the difference and diversity amongst women has yet to be attempted.

The intersection between racial and ethnic exclusion and sexism can be found in a particularly complex and illustrative form in the case of both ethnic employment and familiar labour. It is important to note that this does not tend to be reproduced in the second or third generations however (see Anthias, 1982 and forthcoming; Parmar, 1988) who are indeed much more like their white counterparts in terms of employment than their female relatives and men from ethnic minorities.

In the case of the clothing industry, ethnic entrepreneurs, Asian and Cypriot, play an important role although they are in a subordinate position in relation to the clothing industry as a whole, being in a master/servant relationship to the large contractors (Mitter, 1984; Anthias, 1983; Haringey Employment Project, 1980). Although there are cases of ethnic minority women becoming entrepreneurs (Westwood and Bhachu, 1988) this is relatively rare and men predominate. This is often because they can draw on the cheap or unpaid labour of women from their own families or their own village or ethnic networks (Anthias, 1983). Cypriot women for example are the cornerstone of the Cypriot ethnic economy in North London. Groups that do not present a familialist orientation, like Afro-Caribbeans, have failed to enter small scale business in any significant numbers. As Mitter points out

...the ethic economy throughout the UK is marked by a clear division of labour along gender lines. Unskilled, repetitive, machining work gets done by women – from small units or from home – whereas entrepreneurial skill is practised and monopolised by men (1986: 129).

However, it is important to note that women homeworkers are also found in the low–tech manufacturing industries. The Greenwich Homeworkers Project has pointed to the 'invisible workforce' who make such things as lamp–shades, toys; lick envelopes or fill them; are involved in marketing and selling goods (eg tupperware, catalogues, diets) and increasingly word–processing, clerical work and on computer terminals. New technology has created a new type of homeworker , 'tele–worker' or remote–worker (Mitter, 1984), although it is mainly white women that have been involved or second generation ethnic minority women.

There are a number of issues involved in the case of ethnic entrepreneurs using female labour from their own families and ethnic groups. One is that they have often entered small scale business as a way of avoiding the exclusions and disadvantages they face as migrants and through racism. But in the process, ethnic and family bonds are used to gain class advantages over their own groups and over women in particular. This is not to say that ethnic minority women do not feel that it is advantageous to work for a member of their own group–avoiding racism, language and other cultural problems they face, feeling less alienated. This is well recognised by both workers and employers. For example, Hoel (1982) quotes one Asian employer:

> I see the majority of women working for me as benefitting from my job offer. They are all illiterate and have no skills, hence no British factory will make use of them.

This of course misrepresents the real incorporation of Asian and other women in the manufacturing and service sectors of the economy which we have already referred to.

Ethnic commonality between employer and employee can act to curb participation in trade union activity although small firms in any case are under–unionised (Anthias, 1983). It can however act to undermine class action, thus vitiating the development of class consciousness. For example it is much more difficult to see your employer in class terms when he is a member of your own family. Where there is geographical concentration as in the case of the Cypriot North London community, the face to face interaction between worker and employer extends far beyond the work–place (see Anthias, 1983).

At times ethnic entrepreneurs may employ women from other ethnic groups eg Asian, Afro–Caribbean and Turkish women may be used by Cypriots. In this case ethnic bonding does not emerge but a hierarchy in the work–force with outside women being at times on different piece–rates to ethnic women. This further strengthens ethnic solidarity at the expense of class solidarity amongst women workers.

I have considered ethnic employers and workers and their link not because this is the primary relation that needs analysis in understanding the disadvantages and exclusions that ethnic minority women face – far from it. However, the case of ethnic employment casts an interesting and suggestive light on the intricacy of the link between ethnic class and gender divisions. Class disadvantage can be countered by ethnic or gender strategies, by the use of ethnic resources and commonalities and already established familial ideologies and networks. Ethnic disadvantage (for both men and women) can be countered by increasing or utilising patriarchal gender relations. Ethnic minority women are at the meeting point of the intersection of class, ethnic, and gender disadvantage and exclusion.

Clearly all these factors relating to the specific experiences of ethnic minority women have implications for some of the dominant analyses of women's economic position which have focused on women's role in the family and have seen patriarchal social relations as limiting women's economic participation to part-time work (see Bruegel, 1979, Beechey, 1988). Both the family and patriarchal relations for ethnic minority women do not have the same effect and therefore the nature of causality involved has to be rethought. Moreover the notion of patriarchy assumes that it is relations between men and women that primarily structure women's position (for an analysis of capitalist patriarchy see Hartmann, 1979) but since African–Caribbean women in particular do not exist in such relations of economic dependence vis–a–vis men, this needs reformulation. Similarly the relation of oppression for racialised groups may be one where white or dominant majority women have economic power over minority men and in such cases too the notion of patriarchy is problematised. The idea of the family as the site of women's oppression has also to be rethought as it can be a source of resistance to racism (see Carby, 1982, CCCS, 198).

Cypriot Women and Work

The 'typical' Greek–Cypriot woman in England works either in a clothing firm as a machinist or finisher, as a homeworker, or works alongside and for her husband in the many restaurants, cafés and shops that characterise Greek–Cypriot centres of residence like Haringey in London. There is a tendency however amongst younger women to work in clerical and secretarial work and in hairdressing. Greek–Cypriot women often work for Greek–Cypriot employers and as we argued in the last chapter, were the building block of Greek– Cypriot entrepreneurship.

In this section I will examine the links between sexual divisions at work and the nature of Greek–Cypriot ethnic and economic adaptation.

Data on Cypriot female employment can be extrapolated from the 1971 Census of Population, Economic Activity Tables (10 per cent sample) – the 1981 Census does not include information on Country of Birth and Economic Activity. The major problem here is that there is no specific category for the 'Cypriot' ethnic group who are encompassed under the European Commonwealth category which includes Malta, Gozo and Gibraltar. Although we can assume that the largest proportion of this group are Cypriots we cannot tell how many nor the numbers who are

Greek–Cypriot as opposed to Turkish Cypriot. In addition, the Census categories fail to pick up the economic activity of those born in the UK of Greek–Cypriot parentage and thus we miss an increasingly significant sector. The data are now also out of date. Given these problems, the data we present can only indicate the types of economic activity that Greek–Cypriot women are found in but cannot give precise quantified information.

In terms of economic activity rate, European New Commonwealth women (henceforward referred to as 'Cypriot' for short) are more similar to the total female population (43.5 per cent as opposed to 42.6 per cent for the latter) than to New Commonwealth (49.8 per cent – From OPCS (1971) Country of Birth – Supplementary Tables Vol II). Unofficial estimates of female employment by Greek–Cypriots themselves are far higher than the official ones, ranging from 70 per cent to 90 per cent. The Census data docs not usefully identify home–workers, who often, as we shall see when we examine the Haringey case, have been forced to work illegally or unregistered. In addition, various practices within the Greek–Cypriot Clothing Industry [which employs 66 per cent of Cypriot women according to Clough and Quarmby (1978) although the 1971 Census gives a figure of only 31 per cent] such as the non–formalisation of the employee status of women by employers, lead to women fearing to declare themselves as workers. Local Cypriot community workers have pointed out that a large number of women are told by their employers not to declare their jobs. It is clearly important, then, that we bear in mind these comments which cannot yield any statistically accurate data but indicate tendencies that need to be taken into account in assessing the economic participation of Greek–Cypriot women.

The self–employment rate, as we have noted is high (22.2 per cent) for Cypriot men. For women it is 9.6 per cent. The largest number of employees are clothing workers with 30.5 per cent, followed by Service, Sport and Recreation workers with 22.6 per cent. Clerical workers are the next highest category with 20 per cent.

However, there is a tendency for younger women to work as clerical workers and it is the largest occupational category for the 16 – 20 and 21 – 24 age–groups with 39.9 per cent and 30.8 per cent respectively. The youngest age groups are least likely to enter work as Clothing Workers. The three older age groups have a fairly similar pattern of employment, over a third in each case being Clothing Workers followed by another quarter or so as Service Workers. More of the younger women were likely to be professional and technical workers, the highest proportion being in the 21–24 age group with 12.6 per cent and the lowest being in the 45 – 54 age group with 0.8 per cent

If we break down the economically active female population from the ENCW into industry orders the following picture emerges. Over a half of women are concentrated into Clothing, Footwear and Miscellaneous Services. Clothing and Footwear account for about one third (31 per cent) and Miscellaneous Services for over one fifth (21.8 per cent). The other major employers are Professional and Scientific Services (10.2 per cent), Distributive Trades (9.7 per cent) and Insurance, banking, Finance and Business Services (5.4 per cent). Over one fifth (22.2 per cent) of women are employed in 23 other Industry Orders.

Most women work 'full-time' (over 30 hours per week (70.4 per cent), the largest number working between 36 – 40 hours per week (44.8 per cent of the total) but a significant proportion (16.4 per cent) work over 40 hours per week.

The general picture emerges of a mainly full-time and semi-skilled labour force concentrated in particular sectors of the Economy, such as the Clothing and Service Sectors. These tend to be characterised by small firms and are most vulnerable to fluctuations in the economy (Haringey Employment Project, 1980). It is very likely that a larger number of Greek-Cypriot women work than the data show and that this will be in the Clothing Sector either as 'homeworkers' or unregistered factory workers. In addition many women work alongside and for their husbands in the small cafés, shops and restaurants that characterise Greek-Cypriot localities.

In order to explore more fully women's position at work and their role particularly in the ethnic/economic adaptation of Greek- Cypriots we shall now turn to an examination of the Clothing Industry in Haringey.

Women and the 'Ethnic Economy' – The Clothing Industry

The case of Greek-Cypriot small firms and women's position within them is probably the most relevant in assessing their economic position. Such firms which employ Cypriot women are clothing concerns in Haringey. This is an area where there is a large concentration of Greek-Cypriots.

One of the features of the Clothing Industry is that it is characterised by small-scale factories dependent for production on large-scale companies. The Cypriot clothing firms are not strictly speaking manufacturers but 'outdoor units' or contractors. As the large manufacturers supply them with orders, two problems emerge. Firstly the supply depends in each firm being able to compete successfully for the large manufacturers. Secondly, their supply is subject to fluctuations in the market for women's clothing which is very unstable. Thus, entering the clothing industry always requires the willingness to take on large risks and many small firms close every year, especially during the recent economic recession.

The almost total dependence on orders from large-scale firms and the possibility of these being withdrawn have two effects. One is that small Greek-Cypriot firms, often working with the base-line of full-time employees and relying on a divergent home-working force, attempt to make it work as hard and efficiently as possible to meet rigid submission dates for production. A second is that there is a tendency not to register all full-time workers so that the employer escapes having to pay redundancy when he lays off staff – a common occurrence given the unpredictability of supply of orders from the large manufacturers. The Greek-Cypriot factory employer is himself dependent on a large-scale employer and is the medium by which his fellow-countrymen are exploited, often to ensure his own survival.

The work-force within the Clothing Industry is primarily female. Many firms are located in larger buildings vacated by larger firms who have left London and some are located in previously residential buildings - that is, they are implicated in the urban and industrial decay syndrome mentioned by many writers and a crucial element in Miles and Phizakleas' study of Willesden (1980). Firms rely on employing as small a permanent work-force as possible, depending often on homeworkers who can be easily disposed of, for much of their work.

The location of the factories within Haringey is tied to the geographical distribution and movement of Greek-Cypriots as the Haringey preliminary report on the Cypriot Clothing Industry noted (Haringey Employment Project, 1980). For example the move of this industry from Soho, the East End and Camden Town to Haringey is related to the increasing movement out of these localities of Cypriots themselves. These factories can rely on a source of cheap female 'ethnic' labour which is non-unionised. Women often have little other real choice of work since they lack skills which would enable them to move to different forms of employment, often lack language skills and have few child-care facilities available.

Women who are the mainstay of the Cypriot Clothing Industry are susceptible to high unemployment, low job security and little protection. One of the reasons for this is the failure of the Textile Union to make substantial inroads into the Greek-Cypriot Clothing Industry, and I shall return to the factors limiting the unionisation of the work-force later on. In the following discussion I shall look at the position of women within the Greek- Cypriot clothing industry in order to argue the important role of women in developing the 'ethnic' economy which is central to the particular form that Cypriot ethnicity takes in Britain. I shall also provide evidence for the importance of the mode of economic participation of women in explaining the continuation of female oppression under the supposedly 'liberating' conditions of wage-labour.

As already noted Greek-Cypriot women went into the clothing sector and so did men on the presumption of the skills of women who traditionally made clothes. The entry of Cypriots into this sector is therefore already premised on the skills of women, the needs of women to work in the 'migrant' situation and the over-riding economic motivation for migration.

The earliest employment of women was either in catering with their husbands or in the clothing industry. Partly this was also because they could always from the beginning take out-work which many women needed since it was difficult either to find day-time child-care or get help with children after school. This also suited the employer who thus had a labour-force totally under the control of the demand for labour.

Those who chose to work in the factories where pay was better and employment more regular, often left their children with unqualified childminders many themselves migrants and often caring for five or more small children. For example 'Andrikos', whose parents both worked full-time, in clothing firms (he as a presser and she as a machinist) was left with a baby-minder. She cared for eight small children between 8 am and 9 pm, confining them to one room. This practice, which for parents presented the only child-care opportunity often led to much distress and unhappiness for mother and child.

Within the Clothing Industry there is a sexual division of labour in two senses. Firstly women tend to be employees whereas men are more likely to be employers. Secondly women are usually machinists, finishers or overlockers whereas men are pressers and cutters. Men earn much more than women, the difference being often as much as 100 per cent with overtime. Men however equally face problems of the instability of the industry and often suffer similar results ensuing from the non-registration of the work-force. Men and women are often segregated and are very conscious of the sexual implications of male work-contracts preferring to work with relatives, co-villagers or acquaintances – 'gnostous' where possible. Piece-rate is a common practice for machinists and this again provides the employer with the advantages with the advantage of not having to pay a guaranteed wage especially at times of low output. Women are often unaware of the way in which employers are able to escape their statutory obligations. For example, women are usually paid a net wage without a proper pay-slip. The employer may or may not register her and may or may not pay national insurance contributions which she needs to be properly covered for sickness, unemployment and retirement benefit. A common practice is to declare a low wage and/or low hours of work. Thus women who work – usually 36-40 hours a week or more – may be registered only as part-time workers with all that implies. For example, Maria worked for different Cypriot employers full-time as a finisher from 1967 to 1982, most days working from 9 am to 7 pm and receiving extra payment between 5 pm – 7 pm. This was worked out on the basis of her full-time pay and not at a higher over-time rate. She believed that her national insurance contributions were being paid but when she retired in 1982 discovered she was only eligible for a small proportion of the state pension. Employers also often fail to regard safety regulations. For example, Ellou fell down some concrete steps in her factory and broke her leg. She was thus out of employment for three months and then it took some time for her fully to recover. The employer had failed to provide adequate lighting and thus was responsible. He however denied responsibility, failed to compensate her and indeed sacked her on the grounds that he could not keep her job open until she recovered. It was suggested to Ellou that she should take him to court but she was unwilling as she did not want to create trouble for a fellow 'Cypriot' and 'all the community would find out'. This would lead to her stigmatisation as a disloyal employee and 'Cypriot'.

Women often place more emphasis on the exact amount of net pay they receive than on the conditions of employment, the granting of holiday with pay and the conformity of employers to statutory obligations which are in the interests of their labour force. Indeed, women who are on a weekly wage, may not be allowed time off with pay for sickness, child-care or other reasons. Pay may be deducted at an hourly rate for all absence from work, including lateness. The lunch break may be only half an hour and if the women are on piece-rate many work through it. Women may be laid off before their holiday time is due and employers often close up for 4-5 weeks in the summer months to go back to Cyprus and do not compensate their work-force.

Most Cypriot dress factories are small and enclosed communities, people establishing personal bonds, and the employer-employee relationship is underpinned by ethnic and familial networks. This makes the infiltration of the organised unions very difficult. In any case the networks within the Greek-Cypriot community are such that once a worker becomes identified as a 'disruptive' or 'unionised' element he/she finds it difficult to get work within the 'ethnic economy'. This is true despite the affiliation of many employers and workers to AKEL, the Communist Party of Cyprus and its branch in London (formed in 1974). It is not lack of experience in class struggle that provides the reason for this, but the form that the struggle has been conceptualised in London by the 'progressive' political elements which identifies 'ethnic' capital and 'ethnic' interests as acceptable within the framework of the economic problems faced by Cypriots in the migrant situation. This is also tied to the strategy of AKEL in Cyprus which has always defined the enemy as colonial, foreign or 'unpatriotic' capital but has failed to tackle the issue of indigenous capital and entrepreneurial ideology.

Greek-Cypriot firms are themselves, as noted, dependent on a larger manufacturer and have little capital to fall back on at times of crisis. Their relation to their workers involves an assertion of 'class' interests which is possible on the basis of 'ethnic' loyalty and honour. Cypriot employers and workers often attend the same weddings, may have known each other in Cyprus, often establish 'fictive' kin links where there are no 'natural' ones, and are seen as sharing similar opportunities and disadvantages in British society. In any case the aspirations of the work-force are to be themselves self-employed, and many men often make a transition from 'wage-labourer' to 'small capitalist' within a few years. Profits by small firms are often undeclared so that tax is evaded and Greek-Cypriot accountants are employed who 'cook' the books. The use of 'cabbage' (left over material from the order, made into clothing) provides a retail supply of clothing to the Greek-Cypriot community at much lower cost than in normal retail outlets – one can often buy a 'Marks & Spencer' or 'Richards' equivalent garment at less then half its retail price. Every Greek-Cypriot 'knows' of a factory where this takes place and hence can purchase women's clothing at very competitive prices.

Unionisation has not penetrated into the Cypriot clothing industry. The failure of AKEL, the main left-wing political organisation in London to pursue unionisation is significant. Indeed a number of active AKEL members and those who support it financially are themselves employers. The ethnic interests within the community are seen as more important than any class differentiations. This is partly linked to the common class background of immigrants, self–employed or wage–labour. Most came from the urban and rural displaced population, all finding similar exclusions in British society viz–a–viz language, skill and culture. All share the 'cultural stuff' of the importance of honour, the family and the sexual purity of women. All have a shared experience of British ethnicity via British colonialism. They all see themselves as potential employers and as noted already there is much movement amongst the males in this direction. As regards women we can single out five factors contributing to their unwillingness to organise in the workplace.

(1)   Women do not usually conceptualise the employer as an exploiter for through the dominance of the ethnic category there occurs identification with him. Kin ties and village and social network ties make a class conceptualisation difficult.

(2)   Women themselves are reluctant to organise in Unions because they perceive themselves to have separate interests (from other women) and particular (in relations to men) needs within the Cypriot context. Fear of stigmatisation and disloyalty to the 'friends' – the employer/employee relation often expressed in this idiom – is a major factor here. Women often ask for higher wages and complain as individuals but to organise a movement or within a movement for this purpose is unacceptable.

(3)   Women often 'know' that to jeopardise their job is not worthwhile since opportunities for them outside the Clothing Industry are limited and they prefer the work context of the Cypriot firm. They often do not know to what extent they are disadvantaged in their conditions of employment, since they do not mix freely with other sections of the population.

(4)   Women often feel they get a 'good deal' and often 'boast' of the sums they can make as piece–workers or weekly–waged workers, taking as much as a net pay of £150 – 200 a week. This is often related to the employment of women in Cyprus which is much lower (less than £60 per week on average) and is regarded as quite astonishing despite it often being made up of working long hours under poor conditions.

(5)   There is very little effort within the Greek–Cypriot community to organise women at work. The Left organisations fear losing support if they did so and their members have their own stake as employers. There is also a belief that other openings in the labour market are worse and that it is in the overall interests of the Greek–Cypriot community not to 'interfere' – these interests are defined as those of its males who are the chief 'bread–winners'.

Homeworkers

I have already noted that much female employment in the Clothing Industry is non–enumerated for various reasons. One particular section who fail to appear, more or less, in any official statistics are homeworkers (Allen and Wolkowitz, 1988).

National conditions are surveys of homeworkers are relevant to a consideration of the particular position of Greek–Cypriot women.

Surveys have consistently shown the poor working conditions and pay of such women and the problems involved in their ambiguous employment status. The TUC definition of homework is

> work done in the home for another person, or for sale to another person (TUC – Homeworking, 1977: 2).

The majority of homeworkers are not protected by Trades Union membership; their isolation, insecurity and the small firms involved make this particularly difficult. If they ask for more wages as individuals they may lose their job. The Department of Employment study pointed out

> the most prominent fear was that employers would cut off the supply of homework (Crine, 1981: 8).

They lack employee status, are often defined by their employer as 'self–employed' and thus lack the rights of employees to an itemised pay slip, specified terms and conditions of employment, holiday and maternity leave, redundancy pay or appeal against 'unfair dismissal'.

The distinct advantages to the employer are obvious. Firstly he is not entering a contract with specified obligations and can therefore provide work when and how he chooses and can dismiss the homeworker – if necessary without fearing any ramifications and without compensation. Secondly he is not paying for heating, machinery, lighting or rent – i.e. has no overheads. Thirdly since she is isolated and vulnerable, he can pay her lower rates of pay then a 'normal' employee – she often has little choice but to accept. The majority of women are tied to the home because of child–care and/or domestic responsibilities or through some form of disability or having to care for disabled relatives. When the Commission for Industrial Relations (1974) looked at the Clothing Industry, it found that 55 per cent of its sample were mothers with young children and 15 per cent were caring for sick or dependent husbands. The Survey by ACAS (Advisory Conciliation and Arbitration Service) (1978) found that 58 per cent of workers in the toy industry were women with small children. The DES Survey of October 1980 in the D.E. Gazette says:–

> almost all the homeworkers were women aged between 25 and 44 with dependent children of school age or younger. The choice of home as a place of work was regarded as a sacrifice on behalf of their children (Crine, 1979: 11).

The women themselves are thus constrained by the lack of child–care provision. This is particularly the case for Greek–Cypriot women who may not be aware of whatever limited provisions exist and/or are less willing to search actively for them. Their general lack of skills also makes the choice of part–time work, offering flexible hours, almost non–existent. The ACAS survey of toyworkers shows the wages of homeworkers to be an important source of the family wage and only 18 per cent of those interviewed by CIR (Commission for Industrial Relations) (1974) saw their wage as helping with 'little extras'.

There are various reasons offered by Greek–Cypriot women for homeworking. One is that it allows them to maintain their domestic responsibilities to the satisfaction of an often highly demanding husband and children. Many women say that they like to devote time to tending to their housework, cooking and shopping. The main reason, however, is that many homeworkers, if not most, have dependent children of a pre–school age and either prefer to stay with them at home or indeed cannot find suitable child–care facilities.

Those women who are homeworkers and have small children have often to work from early in the morning to late evening to make a reasonable wage or to finish 'the lot' for the supplier to collect at a specific time. Some women are also so driven by the desire to make as much money as they can, often to be able to buy a house, or buy land or build in Cyprus, or even to buy new furniture (a 'luxurious' house in the 'Cypriot' idiom being always sought) that they exert themselves at great cost to themselves and their children. Often the piece–rate they are on is so low – for example a summer dress can be as little as 50 pence – that they really do work 'all' day to make a reasonable wage. Their children may be left in the house by themselves, perhaps being taken out only for shopping and with the hazards of sewing machine and iron attendant on their play. The sewing machine may be located in the kitchen with its other hazards of cooking and, in the winter, the electric or paraffin heater. Data on the language development of such children is not available but it may be that they start school with two disadvantages. Firstly they may not be able to speak English and secondly they have lacked stimulating play activity and their general aptitude is undeveloped. The provision of pre–school nursery facilities for such children would allow the mother more choice in the type of work she undertakes and allow her children opportunities for language development. The pressures on a Cypriot woman to earn money and at the same time to fulfil her household and child–care obligations, often under the extraordinary demands of a patriarchal male authority who expects his 'Cypriot' meals (often time–consuming to prepare) are tremendous.

Conclusion

I have attempted to outline the role of Greek–Cypriot women in relation to the form that Greek–Cypriot ethnicity has taken in the context of British society. The central role of the economic participation of women in the constitution of the ethnic economy is clear. This participation often involves the extension of the patriarchal relations of the Greek–Cypriot family in the sphere of work.

The propensity for the younger age groups to move into the clerical sphere indicates a move away from the particular form of exploitation of Greek–Cypriot work relations and Greek–Cypriot male entrepreneurship. The extent to which this will reduce the salience of the 'ethnic' category is difficult to estimate, as is the extent to which it will transform the nature of the Greek–Cypriot family and sexual divisions within it. I have argued that economic participation and its forms are crucial elements in understanding the social relations of ethnicity and sexuality.

The next chapter looks at the nature of Greek Cypriot ethnicity in Britain.

7 Cultural identity and the politics of ethnicity

Papoutsin pou ton topon sou j 'an en kommathiasmenon
(A shoe from your own place is better even if torn)
To choma tis patridas einai glykon kai ston thanaton
(The earth of the homeland is sweet even in death)

Greek–Cypriot sayings

Introduction

This chapter considers the political nature of Greek–Cypriot ethnicity in the migrant setting of British society. In particular, the importance given to cultural identity and heritage (religion, language, Cyprus) in the activities of ethnic organisations and their representatives will be examined.

The consideration of ethnic organisation as a form of political mobilisation has a key position in the study of ethnicity and 'race'. There are at least three possible ways in which the link between politics and ethnicity can be made.

(1)   To regard ethnic groups as interest groups, bargaining within a plural society for a greater share of scarce resources
(2)   To regard ethnic actors as striving to promote their individual interests within ethnic organisations.
(3)   To conceive ethnic organisation as facilitating the expression of socioeconomic interests and as a vehicle utilised at specific conjunctures. The consciousness and action of ethnic groups may be different from that of class but intersects with it.

Although ethnic organisation means different things to different people, it is always based on the notion that ethnic origin is a significant arena for cohesion or struggle. But even those ethnic organisations that are formulated primarily around culturalist concerns, may have an integral political function in promoting the class and personal interests of their members within the society of residence. Ethnic organisations are distinct from other cultural or political organisations. Their basis is the ethnic group's separation from the society of origin and from the society of residence; through the territorial separation in the first place and through multi-form economic, social and ideological separation and exclusion in the second case. There is always an incipient politics involved in ethnic organisation, but to reduce ethnicity to politics is as mistaken as to reduce it to class.

Abner Cohen (1969b) provides one of the clearest formulations concerning the political nature of ethnicity. He regards ethnicity as essentially a form of interaction between culture groups operating within common social contexts. This conception does not specify the extent to which ethnicity relates to domination or chauvinism (for example, Orlando Patterson (1977) characterises ethnicity as 'essentially reactionary'). Cohen sees the ethnic group as a form of informal political organisation (interest group) organised around 'collective representations'. The group attempts to advance its interests conceived or represented through these 'symbols'.

Cohen (1969b) maintains that:

> The two types of power, the economic and the political, are certainly different in a number of respects and they are associated with different types of sanctions. But they are intimately interconnected and are in many contexts inseparable. In both, we are in fact dealing with relationships of power between individuals and groups, when these relationships are considered structurally throughout the event of a polity. In both institutions, relationships are manipulative, technical and instrumental, as men in different situations use one another as means to ends and not as ends in themselves (: 217).

He posits the central role of power in the study of all social forms, but this is defined in terms of individual actors coming together in groups in order to further their own individual interests. However, organisation frequently precedes and facilitates the formulation of particular interests (Killian, 1980). These interests will derive in part from the organisational context and even geographical mobilisation of groups and most importantly the possession of organisational tools. Hechter (1975) too believes that given appropriate socioeconomic conditions, a group will engage in collective action only if it has the organisational capacity to do so.

Power relations for Cohen involve 'the dynamics of interaction between men in society.' This reduces everything to the political for in a sense all social interaction is predicated on power relations if this is conceived in terms of the manipulation of symbols. Cohen elsewhere (1969a) shows how the phenomenon called 'tribalism' in contemporary Africa is a result of the increasing interaction of ethnic groups in new political situations after independence.

Ethnicity, as Cohen recognizes is a complex phenomenon involving psychological, historical, economic and political factors. Ethnicity, however, is a vehicle for the construction of a 'difference' upon which inequality might be built. Cohen is rightly critical of those who see

110

ethnicity merely in terms of motivation, primordiality or the psychology of identity, or as a strategy manipulated by individuals to advance their personal interests and maximise their power. The political nature of ethnicity occurs most where there is a high degree of overlap between an ethnic group and other differentiations such as economic and political ones. Cohen makes the distinction between cases where ethnicity coincides with social class and those cases where it extends vertically across it. The former lend themselves to the development of situations where the idioms of ethnicity can be used to express conflict between classes and to further class interests. Where they cross–cut, Cohen notes:

> Manifestations of ethnic identity and exclusiveness will tend to be inhibited by the emerging countervailing alignments of power. The less privileged from one ethnic group will cooperate with the less privileged from other ethnic groups (1974: xxii).

However, elites may use ethnic differentiation to further their own class interests and to undermine the development of horizontal class bonds. Divisive measures, for example, have been used in Cyprus. The construction of divisions between Greek–Cypriots and Turkish Cypriots was facilitated, as I have already argued, by British colonialism.

Although Cohen provides certain insights into the political nature of ethnicity, he faces two particular problems. Firstly, the political is so broadly defined that all social interaction, since it involves a manipulation of symbols, is read as 'political'. Secondly, there is no attempt to analyse forces of domination, state power and economic power and their role in the development of particular forms of political interaction between ethnic groups.

The role of ethnic organisations is multiplex. As Rex (1973) points out they serve to overcome social isolation, to affirm cultural beliefs and values, to foster the attainment of migrant goals and to a greater or lesser extent serve a pastoral function. Rex states:

> And the individual immigrant who knows that there is a man of his own background who has skill in dealing with these problems will go straight to him, rather than to a well–meaning stranger, whom he does not know he can trust (1973).

From this point of view the immigrant needs a cultural retreat where he/she 'knows the rules' and knows that other people accept the rules. However, although such reference points may be essential for the isolated migrant, it is not inevitable that he/she will seek them within the sphere of goal–oriented ethnic organisations as opposed to work or familial relationships. The notion of an essential commonality of psycho–social interests need to be abandoned so that the specific dynamics implicated in the quasi–political organisations of migrants can be addressed.

One argument regarding the revival of ethnicity centres on the idea that with the so–called decline in class allegiances, ethnic communities have taken over their interest group functions. Daniel Bell expresses this point of view succinctly:

111

Ethnicity has become more salient because it can combine an interest with an affective tie. Ethnicity provides a tangible set of common identifications – in language, food, music, names – when other social roles become more abstract and impersonal. In the competition for the values of the society to be realised politically, ethnicity can become a means for claiming place or advantage (1975).

In contrast, Gans (1979) argues that although ethnicity is very much a working–class style in modern America, the resurgence takes the form of a personal response to the alienating tendencies of industrial society and has little class content. Gordon (1978) too, on the other hand, has noted that ethnic identity has come to replace class identity in American society. In Britain, the Ballards (1977) have argued that ethnic consciousness is often a reaction to the racism of modern society and becomes a personal defence mechanism involving the reaffirmation of personal worth. Hall refers to ethnicity as a form of cultural resistance although more recently he has stressed its positive identification elements (1989).

Ethnicity can be conceptualised as a basis for political mobilisation for it relates to a constructed notion of an origin or a history (ethnic culture is its contents) which is considered as a relevant domain of struggle. However, the preservation of ethnic culture and ethnicity (as struggle around an origin) can militate against the expression of heterogeneous class interests. Therefore, although ethnicity involves a political dimension its effects are not unitary – both the class discourse it entails and its concrete effects will be various, contextually and situationally determined.

Greek–Cypriot Ethnicity in Britain

When Greek–Cypriots migrated to England they brought with them an ethnicity that had been formed under specific economic and political processes in Cyprus. (I have already discussed the parallel growth of nationalism and anti–colonialism which contained within them an opposition to both the British and Turkish ethnic category.) The conjunctural and dynamic nature of ethnic processes has been stressed. Greek–Cypriot ethnicity has a history of breaks and discontinuities in Britain. The continuing salience of the ethnic category does not mean the continuation of an already pre–given set of cultural identifications nor that these have the same structural effects.

The view that ethnic orientation is a natural consequence of the value that individuals place on their culture of origin or that it expresses the desire for self–realisation through a search for 'roots' is over–simplified and essentialist.

The Greek–Cypriot 'community' has formed a relatively self–sufficient social system although clearly relying on the State for such essential services as education, health and economic and social regulation. Greek–Cypriots have developed an ethnic economy, based in clothing, catering and retailing and have formed their own political groupings and ethnic associations.

Cypriots are a visible minority, for example, in the Haringey area. Along Green Lanes towards Turnpike Lane Greek–Cypriot shops, banks, cafes and factories announce themselves with Greek signs and names. The black–clothed yiayia (granny) is ubiquitous and the men congregate on the pavements outside the Greek–Cypriot cafes where they play tavli, drink Turkish coffee and read the Greek–Cypriot newspapers – usually Haravgi or Phileleftheros from Cyprus or Parikiaki of London. The Greek–Cypriot household may announce itself with its red painted brick frontage.

In Haringey there is also the Community Centre opened in the early SOs by Haringey Council for use by the Cypriot community. Many social services local offices have Cypriot social workers and there is a strong awareness by the local council of Cypriots as a pressure group. Cypriot grocery stores and supermarkets serve traditional Cypriot food and staples and have now a wide–ranging clientele with the ever–increasing popularity of Greek and Turkish food. Cypriot factories will usually employ Greek–Cypriots and some Turkish–Cypriots and Greek and Cypriot banks will serve Cypriot customers. Doctors, dentists, driving schools, butchers, furniture shops will all serve an ethnic clientele, both Greek–Cypriot and Turkish–Cypriot. Haringey constitutes an ecological centre to the Greek–Cypriot community and ethnic concentration and association are instrumental in perpetuating the ethnic category.

It is interesting to note the differences in ethnic solidarity between the Cypriots and the Maltese who have been studied by Dench (1975). Among Maltese migrants ethnic solidarity is low and goes hand in hand with a low level of both formal and informal association. According to Dench this cannot be accounted for purely by geographical dispersion since Maltese settlement is in several 'moderately sized pockets', although they are a visible minority in only a few streets. Low ethnic solidarity is accounted for by the nature of the migratory flow and the emigration motives of migrants. Migration involved a movement of individuals and not families. The majority of migrants were young single men who were motivated by adventurism and escapism (the 'Capone' element). An additional factor according to Dench was that the Maltese experienced few problems in integrating with the native population and intermarriage was at a high rate of 75 per cent (compared to about 25 per cent for Cypriots). This was also probably linked to the relative absence of Maltese women which may also account for the loosening of religious and ethnic affiliation. Another factor was the ability of the Maltese to move into non–manual jobs and this accounts for 25 per cent of their employment. Cypriots are concentrated in the 'pre–industrial' sectors of catering and clothing (which accounts for 75 per cent of their employment). The Maltese, however, also show a large representation in catering and personal services with 25 per cent here.

Unlike the Maltese, Greek– (and Turkish–) Cypriots desired and were able to maintain their ethnic identity and are a visible community. Cypriots had a strong sense of heritage and ethnicity constructed in Cyprus. They migrated for work and not for adventure. They brought their wives over or if single, married fairly early preferring Cypriot wives.

There is a more or less even sex distribution. Cypriot migration was what is called a 'chain migration'. Cypriots desired to return 'home'. The early ethnic organisations of Greek–Cypriots were built up around the Cyprus problem and were mass organisations (unlike the Turkish–Cypriot ones that tend to be middle–class). Cypriots had a common class background and they used patronage and kinship ties for migration, for employment and for housing. Women too came over to work – as migrant labour. The geographical settlement in London is fairly distinct and Cypriots have developed an ethnic economy (with some elements of an informal economy) which allows them to function as a fairly self–enclosed and independent economic unit within British society.

The Cypriot migrates not for immediate gratification in the country of destination but for economic reasons. This makes him/her more similar to Asian and other New Commonwealth migrants. Cypriots were attracted to Britain because of expanding labour opportunities and the concomitant economic and political uncertainty in Cyprus. Many Cypriots wish to return to Cyprus eventually (they have a 'myth of return') and have orientation to Cyprus. This has consequences for social organisation, class affiliation, and aspiration regarding work and housing. It partly explains the emphasis Cypriots place on capital accumulation and the fact that money is often invested in property in Cyprus. Such investment protects capital from the British tax–man and establishes a base in Cyprus for eventual return.

However, the continuation of this ethnic orientation cannot be explained purely with reference to an idealist identification constructed in Cyprus. For example, the Greek–Turkish distinction became increasingly important in Cyprus in the 1950s as a result of the growth of chauvinist nationalism. Other commentators have noted that the Greek–Turkish distinction is not so relevant in Britain (Ladbury, 1977). The distinct identifications are still relevant but for different purposes. In Cyprus they involved the development of different incipient nation–states and marked economic, religious and linguistic boundaries culminating in geographical separation. In London economic cooperation was induced by the similar ethnic and economic adaptation of Greek and Turkish–Cypriots in their management of a largely sectarian and exclusionary host society. Social interaction between the two communities at an informal level is rare (apart from among the young, born in England). At a more formal level this is more common however. Among the point of contact are the following:

(1) Both Greek and Turkish–Cypriots are entrepreneurial and fill similar niches in the clothing and catering industry. Both bring with them relatively low language and technical skills and the traditional skills and subordination of women that facilitate self–employment.

(2) Both have a highly developed sense of ethnic identity resulting from their political and economic history, social relations of patronage, the importance of the family and sexual purity for women and from religious and traditional modes of action.

(3) Their political activity tends to be oriented primarily round the country of origin or the Turkish mainland (for Turkish–Cypriots) and

there is a polarisation between right–wing and left–wing factions. However, unlike Turkish–Cypriots, the ethnic organisations of Greek–Cypriots are more popularly based – i.e. are not dominated so much by the middle–classes. This may be the result of the historical importance of socialism in Greek–Cypriot social and political life.

Even in 1974, immediately after the coup and subsequent Turkish invasion of Cyprus, there was little disruption to the economic bonds between Greek– and Turkish–Cypriots in London. There were, however, some examples of Greek–Cypriots attacking the shops of those who had supported the right–wing EOKA B. There is no discrimination between the two communities in London and many Greek–Cypriot factories employ Turkish–Cypriot men and women although as Sarah Ladbury (1977) notes it is rarely the other way round.

One possible case of racial discrimination came to the attention of George Eugeniou, the director of the Theatro Technis and Cypriot Advisory Centre in Camden Town. G. Eugeniou was called up by the CCCR (Camden Committee for Community Relations) Officer who told him that some Greek–Cypriot women in a clothing factory had threatened to give notice to leave because there were Turkish (from the mainland) men working as machinists. In Mr Eugeniou's own words, 'Mr Silver started telling us what a good boss he was but these Cypriot women were an ungrateful lot and that he was disgusted with the whole affair; he said that he had been in business for years and he has always employed Cypriot women in his factory and that he has always been very kind to them, trying to help them and educated them at the same time, because his parents were immigrants themselves; they came from Russia and after setting down at the East End, they worked extremely hard, knowing that they have to give a lot in exchange for the opportunities this country offered them; but these Cypriot women are accustomed to taking without giving; he has created wonderful working conditions for them, they had new machines, new toilets (he had to teach them how to make proper use of it, pulling the chain and all that, for they are all peasants you see), he had a modern canteen, he pays them top wages and they are still not satisfied, they are always causing me a lot of trouble, see; I have all sorts of nationalities working for me but I have never experienced any racial discrimination until now, when these Cypriot women came to me offering their resignation, giving me a week's notice to leave. When I asked them why, he carried on, 'because of the Turkish people' they replied; 'As soon as I heard that I got mad; I told them that I will dismiss them immediately on racial grounds and I rang the Ministry of Employment to be on the safe side' he said.

After he had finished his monologue, I asked him whether I could speak to the girls; he agreed and sent a girl to fetch them; then we went to an empty space near the entrance and waited for them to come; after a few minutes they all came, about a dozen of them, both young and old. I explained to them, in Greek, what Mr. Silver said about them not wanting to work with Turkish people. They all denied it. They said that the truth was that they did not like working with men sitting close to them and they had nothing against the Turkish people. Mr Silver said that they were lying because if that was the case, they should have accepted his offer to have them moved to another part of the factory away from the men and if necessary he was prepared to have a 'partition' between them and the Turkish men, but the women refused saying that it wouldn't make any difference since the men would still be on the same floor with them. 'But you have been working with men on the same floor in the past without any objection' said Mr Silver, 'so why do you object now?' he said. 'Yes' said the girls, 'but they were doing a man's job (pressing, cutting, etc.), while these men are doing a woman's job, working as dress machinists. Then Mr Silver asked them if they still wanted to go; some of the girls said yes but the younger ones said that they would like to ask their parents first. 'In that case,' he said, 'I'm giving you all, in the presence of the representative of the Ministry of Employment, instant dismissal'. Then the girls wanted to know whether he would give them any holiday money. 'You'll get what is due to you', he told them. 'I'll send your insurance cards and what is due to you to the Ministry of Labour'. 'No,' said Mr Thomas, you have to send the money straight to each girl's house'. The girls wanted to know whether they were entitled to a week's notice and to some holiday money.

Mr Thomas explained to them that if it was proved that it was a clear case of racial discrimination, then, according to British Law, the employer has the right to dismiss them without giving them a week's notice and not holiday money either.

The Employer then admitted that he had brought the Turkish men from Turkey because he could not get enough Cypriot women to work for him. He was defining the girls' attitudes as racist so he could sack them without having to pay them holiday money.

Ethnic Identity

The orientation of Greek–Cypriots to the British expresses a non–antagonistic but separatist ideology. This is a result primarily of the ambivalence that has been constructed through the relations between Cyprus and Britain. Greek–Cypriot ethnicity was not only anti–colonialist but also contained, as in other parts of the Greek–speaking world, strong elements of cultural superiority. Greek–Cypriots have recognised the greater military, economic and political power of the British but saw them as essentially more culturally and morally wanting. This was often expressed through the low regard of the sexual behaviour of English women, the English family and social values relating to it.

On the other hand, the British presence in Cyprus and 'Westernised' social relations were also epitomisations of a socially valued modern character. The civility and gentility of an idealised English middle–class and the greater opportunities for economic and educational advance in Britain were much admired.

In London, Greek-Cypriot women as early as the late 1950s and early 1960s were able to conform to a Western ideal of womanhood – more groomed, sophisticated and fashionable. Bleaching and undergoing electrolysis for facial and bodily hair were aspects of this. It was not until the late 1960s and 1970s that this trend became apparent in Cyprus, partly through the flow of communication and people between Cyprus and Britain.

Most Greek-Cypriots of the 1st generation witness British social relations from a separatist stance, and have little face-to-face contact with non-Cypriots outside business and official relations. Their knowledge of English culture is gleaned from the T.V. and the popular press and their children's grudging comments from their mainly working-class contacts at school. This is especially true of the older members of the community. Christos (Wimpy Bar Owner – 60, came to England 1945)

> The English are polite aren't they? But they're not the same as us. They don't have strong family ties do they? Their customs are different. I've always got on all right with them though.

When asked whether he had visited any English homes, he said,

> No, I've never been inside their houses. I invite some of my customers to weddings and other occasions. But it's natural to want to mix with your own isn't it?

Andreas (fish-shop owner, 53 who came to England 1958)

> I've never experienced any racial discrimination. But you feel better with your own – you speak the same language in more ways than one. I want my children to stay Greek. I don't like the English way of life.

Ellou (clothing worker in Jewish firm – 49, came to England 1960)

> English women are not good are they? Going out with men even when they're married. I wouldn't want my son to marry one. I get on all right with the English people in the flats, saying hello and talking about the weather. No! I've never been into their flats and they don't come into mine.

The younger ones, especially those under 25 are more likely to have English friends. This is more true of males than females, but even boys, once they leave school, mix with other Greek-Cypriots.
Tony said:

> I don't know why, but most of my friends are Greek now. When I was at school I used to have some English friends. But I go to the Athletic Club with my Greek friends and we go to discos and football matches together.

Young couples tend to live a family-centred life - visiting parents and relations.

Chris and Androulla said: (He has a cafe and she is a teacher in the Greek evening classes)

> Life here is not much fun for Cypriots like us - it's work, work and more work. We don't mix with people. We have so many obligations to our kin on our time off.

Younger professionals will have friendships with non- Cypriots but these tend to remain within the sphere of work. For example, George, Tony and Maria and others have a circle of Greek-Cypriot and Greek friends they associate with.

On the other hand, a few younger ones become more integrated socially. Michael is from Birmingham and he is an active Labour Councillor. He says:

> As a socialist I believe it's important to integrate with the community around you. Cultural differences too often set barriers to real progress.

On the whole, though, left-wing groups in London have links with the British Labour movement but rarely can they establish more personal ties.

Ethnic Identity and Generational Differences

Those who come over to England as adults have a very well-defined ethnic identity. The issue is that of those who came when young or who were born here. One small survey showed that of 95 youngsters born in England, 48 said they were 'Greek' (Cypriot) and the rest said they were a mixture of Greek/English (Parikiaki Haravgi, November 1981). In another sample, 42.9 per cent (of all age groups) said they were Greek-Cypriot; a further 31 per cent said they were Cypriot, a small number said British or mainly British (6 per cent) and 'Greek and Other' accounted for 3.6 per cent only. (Leewenberg, 1979: 58).

One teacher (Parikiaki Haravgi, February 1982) in the community schools in London conducted a survey of 108 pupils who were over 14 at the Community Schools. 90 of his sample identified themselves as Greek/Cypriot with 17 as British/Cypriot and 1 as British. Of these, interestingly enough, as many as 38 said they would like to settle down in Cyprus eventually, only 28 wanting to do so in England (the rest choosing 'elsewhere' or 'didn't know'). I shall return to the issue of the young later on in this chapter.

This is a typical response of the older Cypriot. Pavlos, a man of 60 was very clear about his ethnic identity:

> I came over when I was 23 and I didn't like it at first. The weather was so bad and it wasn't the same as Cyprus, knowing everyone and all that. But I worked hard - it was terrible in those days, working 12 hours a day to earn £2 a week. I gave it up and went to Cyprus but I couldn't get a job over there and came back. I'll go back one

day. I've got a little flat in Larnaca which I let out. My kids are all working now apart from my eldest son who is studying Civil-Engineering. My daughter's a trained designer but she can't get a job in that field so she's working in a shop. She said 'Dad, I'm going to come and work with you when you've sold your fish shop'. My younger son helps me – he said it's better this way – he's more free. I'm going to start a dry–cleaning business if I can sell my fish shop.

This man was questioned about his children's education and felt that those who were more integrated and active in the community were more likely to stay at school and do well. Pressures at school led to children leaving early though. However, a Greek–Cypriot woman of 35 who came over at 10 years of age said:

Cyprus is like a dream to me now. All my roots are here. My mum and dad and brothers and sisters. My husband's the same. But we would go back and give it a try if we could set up a little business. I love the weather and the slower pace of life.

One pressing effect for the economic migrant with a homeland orientation is the lack of motivation to learn the language of the society of residence, or acquire a training (which might mean a loss of income). In London, especially, it is not absolutely necessary to learn good English as there are work openings in Greek–Cypriot small establishments and there exist an abundance of social activities within a self–contained Greek–Cypriot idiom. This, of course, does not mean that Greek–Cypriots do not experience structural disadvantages from lack of language or training skills, merely that their own motivation to acquire them is contained by their identification so closely with their own ethnic category.

Another effect of such economic migration is that Greek–Cypriots do not become integrated into the political and organisational world of British society. They rarely actively participate within the main political parties (they join their own which are oriented to Cyprus), although the majority are Labour supporters. It also result in a 'cash– nexus approach and Cypriots may fail to consider the quality of life or job satisfaction or the number of hours they work. This may mean sacrifice in time with their children, in the pursuit of leisure, in active involvement in organisations.

Greek–Cypriots work hard, working long hours to give a better life to their children and for an eventual return to Cyprus. As far as eventual return is concerned they may purchase property in Cyprus which both exempts them from taxation burdens, but also fulfils their aspirations for a base in Cyprus. These tendencies towards a monetary inclination also have wide–reaching effects on Cyprus as a whole for every Cypriot village in Cyprus has a relative or a friend in Britain who will visit Cyprus and display their relatively greater economic affluence. Cypriots in London and in Cyprus, for some purposes, have to be seen as part of a unified whole – a Greek–Cypriot identification and orientation, although clearly the broader social relations within which they are inserted differ considerably.

119

The early economic adaptation of Greek–Cypriots within the structural constraints imposed by the British labour market and their own lack of skills and language led to the development of a self–employment ethic and a relatively autonomous Greek–Cypriot mode of economic activity that has helped to foster the ethnic category. In addition the role of Greek–Cypriot women is important in the perpetuation of the salience of ethnicity (as already discussed in the last two chapters). The geographical concentration of Greek– Cypriots, their common class backgrounds, the role of kinship and friendship networks in migration, mobilisation around the Cyprus problem and a cultural division of labour are all important.

British–born Cypriots and Ethnicity

There is continuing identification with being Cypriot amongst the young, although when asked in English they spontaneously reply they are Greek. If asked in Greek, they will reply they are Cypriot. This is linked to two elements. Firstly, the language spoken is Greek and, therefore, this provides them with the best identity marker in England. Another is that 'Cypriot' denotes in England both an ambiguous identity (Turkish–speaking or Greek–speaking) and also a more 'lower–class' depiction. Most young people, however, express a certain degree of ambivalence about their ethnic identity, although they often 'know' they are Greek/Cypriot 'deep down'.

The main factors for identity maintenance for all age groups are seen to be the effectivity of the Cyprus problem the economic, geographical and social organisation of Cypriots and the attitudes of the English that are seen by many as antagonistic to foreigners. Many youngsters go through a stage at school of rejecting their Cypriotness but returning to it later as they became more aware of the difficulties of integrating economically and socially in British life and the problems they face as foreigners. To many also their ethnic category can facilitate employment. Young men especially may choose to work with their fathers in shops, cafes and factories or work for other Cypriots. The girls are more likely to move away in term of employment, preferring clerical or other white–collar work, hairdressing or fashion designing (this last appears an upward trend).

The ambivalence of the young about their identity is expressed by Nikos, 25, who was born in England and works as a presser. He says:

> I feel a bit strange when I go to Cyprus because they all think I'm really weird as I don't speak Greek all that well. But I'd love to go back and live some day. I like the beaches and the sun. I feel I belong there more than here. Mind you, after I've been there a few weeks I miss my friends over here and especially the football. You've got more freedom in England. Also in Cyprus they call me Englezoudi (little English boy) which upsets me.

Some British–born Cypriots idealise the Cyprus they have visited on holiday and want to return to live there. Androulla (22) has taken her

'English ways' and her smart fashions and English/Greek accent to Cyprus. She is staying with her uncle in Larnaca and his family, although they are afraid of her 'ways', and are pressing her parents to bring her back to England. Her parents now say that she must return after two months until the whole family can go back to live there. Androulla wants to marry a Greek-Cypriot and concerted efforts are being made in Cyprus to find her a 'kalo pedi' (good boy) to marry.

As British-born Cypriot men leave school and even college, a proportion will actively choose to return to more traditional employment – self-employment. Yiannis is a case in point.

Yiannis was born in England, his father has a small transport cafe in Camberwell which he runs with his wife (he is the cook, his wife serves the customers). Yiannis spoke mainly English while at school and despised Cypriots and though they were 'peasants' and 'bigots'. He did well enough at school to go to Polytechnic where he took a degree in Economics. During this period he consciously avoided mixing with other Cypriot students and made many English friends. However, during his studies he was obligated to his parents and helped them in their cafe. His father bought him a flat over a hairdresser' shop and his brother took this last over. Then he and his brother began a business venture in holiday flats in Cyprus. In 1974, with the coup and Turkish invasion, Yiannis became fiercely involved in the activities within the Cypriot community in London and came, not only to acknowledge his roots but to be proud of them. Soon afterwards he met a Greek-Cypriot teacher and married her. For almost a year he worked as a civil servant but at the same time helped his father-in-law in his Steak House at evenings and weekends. He then took over its management and is now permanently involved in business and the Cypriot idiom it involves. He has few English friends and leads a family and community centred life.

This phenomenon is not unique. The factors in Yiannis's case were related to his great ambivalence towards being a Cypriot and his early denial of his family and culture or origin. Subsequently these became a resource he could draw upon economically and emotionally. To remain Cypriot is preferable for him given access to business within the Cypriot community which yielded more income, satisfaction and identification than his civil service job. However, he also feels that he has sacrificed wider cultural and social involvement and almost all leisure. Even where British-born Cypriots may speak English better than Greek, like Yiannis, they are still ethnic in the sense that their social relations are bound by the form of economic and social adaptation of their families within a new and exclusionary social context.

It is frequently claimed that the young are 'caught between two cultures' which has psychological/personal effects. But they also experience problems of minority status which involves exclusion from certain forms of knowledge (how to play the system) which may be similar to underprivileged sections of the working class. In addition, there is dissonance between parental modes of behaviour and those at school and youngsters may see themselves as 'doubly misunderstood'. Parents may

121

refuse to allow the young to negotiate their identity and culture in Britain. The school may not understand their specific, culturally and structurally related, behaviour and may see them as problems. Boys will rebel more at school than girls who are more conformist. Girls, however, face special problems as a result of different values and expectations from their peers and the school and the rigid sexual values of their parents. Generally, Greek–Cypriot girls are restricted by their parents, are not allowed to go out with non–Cypriot girls and most of them are not allowed to have boyfriends. Friends at school will boast of the boys they have been out with and the discos and pubs they have been to. Cypriot girls will feel outsiders (this is equally true of Greek– and Turkish–Cypriots) and so, not surprisingly, will make friends with each other. Cypriot girls, both Greek and Turkish, will mix freely for they have much in common in their subjection to rigid sexual mores. Girls, however, do respond differentially and find their own methods of managing the disparate expectations of them. When they leave school the dissonance will diminish.

Yianna (21) says:

> We have problems with our parents about going out. They don't like us to go out with English girls even. I remember many fights with them when I was at school. It made me feel very different and excluded when I couldn't go out to the pictures or discos with my mates at school. I don't mind so much now. I've got lots of Greek friends. I do sometimes go out with boys but my parents don't know it. I keep it secret because they would fly through the roof if they knew. I do believe girls should be virgins and I would like to marry a Greek boy but if I loved an English boy I would marry him.

Anthoulla is married to an English fellow student. She says:

> When I met Dave I didn't tell my parents about it. But my brother knew and thought it was alright. I don't really get on with my mum and dad. My dad's the worse, he thinks that Englishmen don't know how to treat a woman properly. But they have come round to the situation now and accept us both.

Dina is a student of 23 and says:

> I'd really like to marry a Greek boy. I think I've got much more in common with Greeks. For example, we're a lot more friendly and outgoing than the English. But I don't want to have an arranged marriage really. On the other hand, if my parents introduce me to someone nice then I'd be pleased. I don't want to stay on the shelf. I'll probably end up marrying an Englishman because Greek boys look down on you if you go out with them. It's all right for English girls, they'll respect them – but if you do they think you're cheap and won't want it to become serious.

One boy told of his experience in going out with Greek–Cypriot girls.

> There was this girl: She was a lot older than me and she kept on giving me the eye when she came into my dad's shop. Anyway, she

was nice–looking and I went out with her twice and then went to bed with her. I'd already told her what's what – that I wasn't ready for marriage or anything – but the next I heard of it was her dad on the 'phone threatening to come and beat me up if I didn't get engaged to her. I told him where to get off but my dad eventually had to have a good word with the girl's dad before he stopped. That's the trouble with Greek girls – all they want is to catch you.

Christina felt that Greek girls were often hypocritical and things had changed a lot.

Most Greek girls are out for what they can get – nice clothes, a car, some money from their parents. But on the quiet, they'll do anything (i.e. have sex with boys).

The arranged marriage is by no means common and marriage in Church is more or less mandatory. A custom deriving from the Greek–Cypriot community in England is the pinning of money on the bride which has spread to Cyprus. Wedding feasts are large and are often held in Town Halls. For the better–off, hotels providing seating for 300 or more guests are common – similar to the entrepreneurial Jewish community in London. Some girls prefer it this way:

Katerina (22) a bank clerk, said:

I respect my parents and their customs. I really admire them and think I'm better off in my family and culture than most English girls. My parents would do anything for me. I'm really happy not to be like English girls. They get so twisted up having sex with boys. I want to get married when I'm 23. I'd like to meet someone or my parents to find me someone pretty soon.

Boys too respond differentially. However, the differences can be much larger here. Some boys will join gangs and experiment with crime and drugs but this does not occur to a large extent. The class differences in the young are important for they facilitate exposure to certain youth sub-cultures. In Haringey there is a tendency for some children of factory and shop workers to identify with the youth subcultures around them and reject parental values and authority. These are often the children of those who are not involved in ethnic organisations and who became more anomic. Problems of housing, work and depression are more common in this group.

A second tendency is found amongst those who identify strongly with their ethnic category, generally after a period of rejecting it at school. These are the children who are sent to Greek classes and clubs – many of them the sons of shopkeepers and/or organisational activists. This is also true for girls.

Finally, there is a small group who move away from Cypriot identity and social life. They are more likely to have 'made it' in the educational system – that is, have achieved extremely good examination results and have become professional workers of one type or another – lecturers, artists or doctors. However, not all such achievers lose their ethnic identity.

I shall now turn to looking at the more clearly political aspects of ethnicity including ethnic organisations.

Religion

The Greek Orthodox Religion constitutes an important feature of ethnicity for Greek-Cypriots although their orientation can be characterised as passive religiosity. The earliest nationalism used explicitly religious articulations as opposed to secular ones. Turkish-Cypriots on the other hand, under the influence of Kemalism developed a more secular and Statist ethnic identity. Most Greek-Cypriots in Britain maintain the traditional religious festivals, the most important being the following:

Christmas –	Nistia (Fasting) Sausages made
New Year –	Ayhios Vasilis (St. Basil) Break of fast Vassilopitta (Basil's cake)
Easter –	Flaounes (Cheese and Fruit Pies), Nistia (fast) Epitaphios
At all times –	Weddings, Baptisms, Funerals, Remembrances

Older women are usually the mainstay, economically, spiritually and practically of the Church. Women of all ages will attend Church on the above occasions, taking their children with them to the 'kinonia' (communion) before they break the fast. Men go less frequently.

Although religion has been recognised as important in constructing boundaries and in defining the culture world or mode of thought in society, neither religious involvement or religious ideology for Greek-Cypriots plays as important an ethnic/political role as it did in Cyprus (compared also to the rise of Muslim fundamentalism within Britain's Asian communities).

The Greek-Orthodox Church in Great Britain has had a significant political role, however. It has a long history dating from 1676 when a colony of Greeks settled in Soho. The Aghia Sophia Church was built in Moscow Road, Bayswater in 1879. The All Saints Church was opened by Greek-Cypriots in a former Anglican Church in Camden Town in 1948. This was followed by others, both outside London and in those boroughs where Greek-Cypriots live, such as Camberwell, Hendon, Wood Green, and Hackney to name but a few. The Church in Britain has always been dominated by Greek priests from the mainland and has usually propagated nationalist, rightist and chauvinist views. It set up the first Greek classes before the Second World War. The Church is an important focal point for the non-organisationally minded community. The more left-wing Community activists on the other hand, are usually not such ardent attenders.

Eftihia who is 60 years old and has lived here since 1958 says:

It is good for me to go to our Church. God is good and he looks after us in our exile. You must follow the traditions of your faith. Faith is very important. The true Greek must also be a true Christian.

Panikkos who is 45 years old and has lived here since 1961 said:

I'll go to Weddings and Funerals but I don't believe in all this 'Kyrie-Eleyson' of the old women. I do believe in God though. Of course, I've baptised my children, otherwise they won't be 'Christian' will they? Anyway, I'd like to go and live in Cyprus eventually. My wife feels the same. I don't hold with all these customs – they're a bit backward, aren't they?

Language and Ethnicity – Struggles Around Language

Another important element of Greek-Cypriot ethnicity is language and struggle around language. Language plays a different role at various stages of ethnic mobilisation. According to Taylor and Giles in 'Language and Ethnic Relations' (1979) language is more than an indicator of ethnicity, it is fairly central to the creation, definition and maintenance of social categories.

Asked about language maintenance the following response by a 50 year old man was typical

It's good to keep your language. It's a beautiful language anyway. I get angry when my kids don't speak it. It makes me feel I've lost my way. It's important to keep your culture – we are Greek and weren't they the first civilisation – the envy of the world? I speak Greek at home but my kids answer me, usually, in English.

Another man (52) said:

As long as my kids can speak it when they go on holiday to Cyprus I don't mind if they speak English most of the time. It's natural for them isn't it? I'd like my kids to marry Cypriots then they will have more in common with us too and we can all stay together and understand each other.

Greek-Cypriot ethnic mobilisation in Britain has not been around specifically class issues or economic interests but around language maintenance which is regarded as central to preserving ethnic identity. One of the largest Greek-Cypriot organisations is the Greek Parents' Association which is affiliated to OESEKA (Union of Greek-Cypriot Educational Organisations in Britain).

The Greek Parents Association was formed in 1952 at the same time as the establishment of the first Community School which was opened in Camden Town. The Association led by Tefcros Anthias, (the well-known Cypriot poet) with the help of left groups, were able to buy a detached villa. Entrepreneurs helped to finance it, through their donations, and members personally collected funds. A Greek-Cypriot gave all his savings and occupied the top flat in the building. The first school saw its aims as perpetuating Greek language and culture – it taught folk–dances, songs and customs and many plays were performed by children. In the early days, the events were packed. Most community schools are now under the aegis of the Association which is non–sectarian.

In 1968 the Greek–Cypriot community asked for help from the Cypriot Government in organising the teaching of Greek and fostering the ethnic identity of children born or being brought up in England. In August 1969 the first Cypriot educational mission came over with five teachers and one inspector. The mission, however, suffered attacks from the Greek junta that was in power in Greece and its representatives in Britain, the Greek Embassy and the Church hierarchy. With the aim of taking the mission over, ten Greek mainland teachers were sent over in 1970 under the aegis of Archbishop Athenagoras. Thus a schism widened within the educational organisations of the community. The Cyprus Government in 1972 was forced to withdraw its educational mission. The Greek Government gave much financial support to the Church schools. In 1976 the second Cypriot educational Mission was sent over with eighteen teachers from Cyprus and this practice has continued. The classes are housed in English schools. OESEKA's concerns (formed in 1970) are to improve the conditions of the Cypriot community, to teach the language, culture and traditions of Cyprus, and to teach the ancient and modern history of Greece and Cyprus. Recently (1990) an umbrella organisation has been formed under which all Greek–language provision is encouraged. The Church schools are directed by the Greek Orthodox Church, paid for from Greece and reflects the nationalism of Greek texts. There is, in fact, no set curriculum and what is taught will depend on the particular teacher. Some of the teachers are provided by the Cyprus Educational Mission.

Pupils' attendance of community schools is often under duress from their parents and many children say they find them boring. As they get older they tend to appreciate them more however. Many pupils go on to take Modern Greek GCSE and 'A' Level GCE. Pupils will speak a mixture of English and Greek but as they get older, especially if they go regularly to Cyprus on holiday, they will value speaking Greek and develop their aptitude for it. For example, when Eleni was at school she did not take an interest in the Greek language but in her late teens she taught herself to read and write and now speaks Greek quite well although with an English accent. Often the Greek spoken is the Cypriot dialect and this makes it difficult for Greek teachers from the mainland to understand the children. The combination of dialect, English accent and English words being interspersed lead them to believe that the child has lost its Greek. But this is generally not the case.

Pirkko Elliot's (1981) study of some Greek mother–tongue classes reveals that pupils are encouraged at home despite teachers often regarding parents as 'wanting to get rid of their children' while they attend to their business activities. Children many attend as many as three classes a week (between 6 and 8pm) and then stay on to the club that follows the class until 9.30pm.

126

The debate on whether to introduce mother-tongue teaching in the primary and secondary school state sector (which related to the EEC recommendations) prompted or added weight to the demands of ethnic organisations. One criticism made of the introduction of mother-tongue teaching in the school curriculum was that it could lead to the disbandment of the voluntary sector and that this would deprive language of its pressure-group political dimensions. Another argument was that mother-tongue teaching as a formal aspect of the state sector could detract from the school's concern with fostering achievement of the immigrant child within those areas most relevant to social advancement in the country of settlement.

Some Greek-Cypriot children feel that they are even more differentiated through mother-tongue provision from the 'native' children and resent being singled out for special treatment. Some children already feel earmarked by their foreign-sounding names, their parents' appearance, behaviour and heavily accented and broken English. They may not inform their parents of school Open Days because they are embarrassed by them. In addition, parents may not be encouraged enough by the school to attend and schools do not adequately explain the function of school events. Some Mothers, who are less likely to speak English, find it difficult in any case to communicate and will have to rely on their child to translate the teacher's remarks and to inform the teacher of any anxieties they may have concerning their child. Fathers may be too busy working unsocial hours or may believe in leaving education to the 'expert'.

Clearly, language maintenance is an important aspect of identity but the ethnic element is neither a necessary development from language nor does it require it although it will facilitate it. Many children who barely speak Greek are still inserted within the social relations of their parents' ethnicity and will develop a distinct Cypriot idiom in their English language and accent as well as having a Cypriot identity.

Political Organisations

When considering the constituent elements of Greek-Cypriot ethnic organisation, it is necessary to point out that they have different explicit objectives and functions – for example, some are political, others are cultural and yet others are community action based – all of them, however, are community associations of migrants and have particular effects from the migrants point of view, although they are not all explicitly goal-attainment organisations.

As far as Greek-Cypriots are concerned there has been the development (in addition to those that have an explicitly political role in relation to country of origin) of more interest-oriented ethnic organisations. Their orientation is to the British state and they are in a process of negotiation with it. This is linked to the growth of concern by the state with ethnic minorities and the provision of funding for mother-tongue teaching and community and advisory centres.

One of the striking features of political organisations and the publications of the Greek–Cypriot community is the extent to which political affairs in Cyprus – the Cyprus problem – dominate.

The political organisations of ethnic groups are ethnic organisations in their most clearly political expression. For the Greek–Cypriot community in London in particular the earliest organisations were political ones. This is related to the polarity in Cyprus itself between the right and the left and the strong allegiances that Greek–Cypriots brought with them. In addition, it relates to the dominance of Cypriot political life on Cypriot consciousness which is the result of both the particular construction of Cypriot ethnicity which we noted in Chapter 3 and the continuing effects of the Cyprus problem or the national issue. It also, both structures and exemplifies the home orientation of Cypriots.

The first Cypriot political organisation was Adelphotita (the Greek–Cypriot brotherhood) which has a right wing base. This was established in 1934 by the Archbishop in London and functioned as a meeting place and social retreat for the earliest migrants – it offered help in finding work and accommodation and a place to read newspapers and eat Cypriot food. In the evening there was some teaching of English.

Adelphotita saw its main task as the preservation of ethnic identity and providing help for Cyprus. It wanted to dominate the Cypriot community before the left–wing and was not oriented particularly to British social life. It had and still has links with the Church and the Cyprus High Commission. However, it did not have a wide–ranging influence on Greek–Cypriot workers who were more concerned with their economic problems nor did it ever take the initiative in developing interest groups vis–a–vis the British State (although it was involved in national protests). It relied on independent funds and donations and had political and financial help from Greek–Cypriot right–wing forces. The student body was more active and competed more effectively for community support but this was later dissolved. Adelphotita has become more 'progressive' (sic) however, over time and there is more unity with other groups.

In the 1930s Left groups were formed and there was a Cypriot section of the British Communist Party. In the 1960s the special Cypriot section of the Communist party of Great Britain was disbanded and some of the leading members of the Cypriot section think that such a move was long overdue. It was argued that the existence of a separate section led to insularity from British struggles. But it is probably true to say that Cypriots would have found it difficult to join British local groups because of the language problem.

AKEL (the Communist Party of Cyprus) set up a London contingent in 1974. The extent of membership is not as relevant as the impact of the ethnic organisation on the ethnic community and the society of residence. This is specially pertinent for the left organisations. They were more instrumental in developing management strategies in London – that is through fostering schools, youth clubs, women s associations, residents' associations, theatre groups, clubs, dancing classes etc. Important for these were the ethnic symbols and the class element – which informed the management strategy – may have become subordinated over time. This is reflected in the persistent inability of these groups for example to tackle issues of unionisation within the community. Unionisation has clearly been limited by the involvement of many left group members in self–employment. This, also to some extent, explains the failure of the left to tackle this issue. Where the newspapers, Vema (now defunct) and Parikiaki are concerned there was some fear that advertisers would stop publishing in the newspapers and thus deprive them of needed revenue. The individualism inherent in the workings of the ethnic sub–economy, which involves certain elements of what has been termed an informal economy, has rarely been tackled. The activities of the Left, however, in interplay with the latest phase of the race relations industry have been instrumental in setting up the Cypriot Advisory Centres at Holloway, Camden, Hackney and Wood Green which have recently (mostly in the last ten to fifteen years) been established.

Most political organisations are primarily concerned with the Cyprus problem and pay little attention to questions of British politics. Both the right and the left organisations are represented in ESEKA (Coordinating Committee of Greek–Cypriots in England) which was formed in 1974 after the Turkish invasion in Cyprus. This unifies them in their concern for a solution to the Cyprus problem and has done much to lessen sectarianism within the Cypriot community.

There are various other organisations that express more universalistic aims, however. Theatro Technis is one of them, built with the hard work of a few men and women led by George Eugeniou. This is a progressive theatre and also has an advice centre instigated by its leader. It runs a service for the old and was very important in forming a pressure group for refugees from Cyprus. Its advisory centre deals with about 8,000 cases per year – especially work problems, housing, social security and so on.

Theatro Technis relates both to the Turkish–Cypriot community and an English audience. It has specific class goals using the medium of ethnicity as a resource and is concerned with depicting the Cypriot experience in dramatic form.

Since 1974, a large number of village based organisations have been created which are particularly important for those whose villages are in the Turkish controlled part of the island.

The Local Residents' Associations (of which Haringey and Enfield are the largest) are concerned with community interests and are non-sectarian.

The Youth Clubs provide a forum for the young to meet and to learn the traditions of their country of origin. This has a useful role in bridging the cultural no–mans–land that many youth find themselves in. The British state has provided support for those community–based organisations that were most dynamic in the 1950s through urban aid programmes and finance from local boroughs. The Schools Council's project was especially important since it was part of a programme to introduce Greek into the normal school curriculum (late 70s and early 1980s). The local Community Relations Council in Haringey has a Greek–Cypriot and a

Turkish–Cypriot officer and there are Greek and Turkish–Cypriot Liaison Officers. Recognition has thus been given that Cypriots are a minority migrant group and like Asians and Afro–Caribbeans need the support of the State and sensitivity to their particular problems.

The Greek–Cypriot Press in London

The Greek–Cypriot newspapers play a very important role in the community and are widely read. Vema, at one time (before its demise in the mid–80s) was the most popular with a readership of 8,500 in 1982. Vema was founded in 1939 by a group of Greek–Cypriot communists tied to the Communist party of Great Britain (CPGB). Papaioannou ('Papis' – General Secretary of AKEL in Cyprus (the Communist Party) for many years), Eudoras Joannides (otherwise known as Doros Alantos the well-known writer) and Tefcros Anthias (the well-known poet and socialist/humanist) have all been past editors of Vema. Its most recent editor was George Pefkos (since 1964).

Parikiaki Haravgi (edited by the well known left–wing journalist, Kyriakos Tsioupras) first came out in 1974 (after and as a response to the 1974 coup and subsequent Turkish invasion in Cyprus). It is the party organ of AKEL in London and first appeared with the formation of a London– based contingent. Its existence highlights the extent to which Greek–Cypriot political leaders believe that political work around the Cyprus problem is important in London and the enormous and continuing links of Cyprus and London for Greek–Cypriots. Other Greek–Cypriot parties of all colours have established a London office such as The EDEK (Socialist) party of Lyssarides and the Rally (Right–wing) party of Clerides. London appears not only as a natural extension of Cyprus but political developments in London amongst the community are often mirror–images of political life in Cyprus. Parikiaki, as it is now called, is the most significant community newspaper – others come and go – and about 15 papers have started up and disappeared in the last 30 years. Since Vema's demise in the mid–1980s Parikiaki has had an English section and has tried to attract a British–Cypriot audience by also paying more attention to the experiences and difficulties faced by the British–born Cypriot. The Community Radio (London Greek Radio) legally started in the late–1980s also provides an important service to the Cypriot community and its impact on ethnicity has yet to be assessed.

Identity Politics and Ethnic Provision

In the recent race relations policy of funding for ethnic minorities, getting access to resources by groups has generally meant classifying oneself under the rubric of disadvantage. However, because racist 'disadvantage' is integral to all sections, those who are most likely to be funded as representatives of the disadvantaged groups are the more traditional groups (Anthias and Yuval Davis, 1992). Such groups tend to be cultural groups who are seen as more credible in representing often stereotyped views of the character and needs of the ethnic group.

However, this process is far from clear cut. Where traditional leaders of the ethnic community in question have failed to provide an organisational forum for younger more dissenting voices the principle of funding groups on the basis of special needs has often helped to empower them. For example, the traditional leaders have tended to be reluctant to take advantage of these policies not defining themselves under the rubric of racially disadvantaged groups. Their sights are set on issues of maintaining the ethnic identity of the young and the ethnic cause in the homeland. However, British born Cypriots have found it difficult to have their views effectively expressed and listened to, views on the problem of ethnic identity and the maintenance of culture that threaten the older more established leadership. With the new phase of race relations policies, the young British born Cypriots have been able to manipulate the symbols of English culture and formed their own groups. There has occurred a growth in young women's groups for example. Young people have begun to fill posts as youth and community workers and outreach workers for local councils and have directly challenged the traditional leaders. However, such groups and aims remain marginal.

The more traditional leaders are concerned with the maintenance of ethnic identity, stressing the role of common origin and the retention of culture. By this they mean not only a love and concern for Cyprus but the upkeep of language, religion, and sexual and familial values, of customs and traditions. These have been kept in a type of time warp, a phenomenon that can be understood as a closure process in relation to threats of extinction in an alien and largely hostile culture. These traditions and attitudes are held on to in a more entrenched way than in Cyprus, where they have naturally developed in accord with other social and economic changes.

The younger activists on the other hand want to build a Cypriot ethnicity that shares an ethnic minority identity with Turkish Cypriots and other 'black' groups. They are more concerned with stressing the commonality of experience in a racist society. In this process they are rejecting a culturalist form of politics in favour of an ideological stand against racism. However, the difficulty they face in this enterprise relates to their failure to enter the black community on the one hand, and their object of reference being an attempt to build a new Cypriot identity. A general problem appears to be that once the issue of the centrality of the groups identity comes in to play its point of reference becomes the community that it is outside. If British born Cypriots cannot really belong to 'The Community' (either British or Cypriot) then they can only be part of the communities of disadvantage to be subjected to corrective action. It is not so much that they are between two cultures (sic) but become visible only as a category of corrective action which asks them for credentials of belonging to the authentic Cypriot culture. This has not posed much of a problem because the traditional leaders have been able to gain the bulk of funding although a well organised community centre and have left special projects to the young. How satisfactory this will be for the British born Cypriot is unclear for they most of all want to redefine the ways in which they can be Cypriot in British society, which is something positive rather than merely negative.

Class Divisions Within the Greek–Cypriot Community

Class polarisation among Greek–Cypriots in Britain is less clear–cut than in Cyprus, largely because of the predominance of unskilled and semi–skilled workers and peasants amongst those who migrated. However, since the 1960s there has been an increase in the numbers of educated and professional people, some through participation in the British higher education system but others through the various missions and concerns of the Cyprus High Commission in London. In terms of the distinctions made by Cypriots themselves, there is a separating out of this group as having special status.

Cypriots in London may also distinguish themselves from each other on the basis of amount of money or capital accumulated and whether they have been successful in business which in turn is seen as linked to the locality in which they live. For example, those in Haringey are more likely to be seen as 'horkates' (peasants) by those in Hendon and in turn the latter are seen often as 'pseudo–aristocrats' by the Haringey inhabitants.

However, despite these evaluative distinctions based on economistic criteria, it is often political divisions which are most important, these usually coinciding with familial, village friendship and organisational networks. However, the importance of these political divisions will usually themselves depend on developments in the Cyprus problem which unites the ethnic dimension. The best example of this is the way since the 1974 Turkish invasion of Cyprus, the Coordinating committee of Cypriots which was set up (ESEKA) united political grouping and mitigated the sectarianism that had often characterised relations between the active left and right members of the community.

For the ordinary Cypriot the ethnic dimension informs more his/her personal relations and attitudes than any strong class divisions within the ethnic group. For example, in Cyprus, cafeneion society (a masculine domain) is separated into right–wing and left–wing cafes where the men congregate, drink coffee and discuss politics. In London this division does not hold to the same extent and political differences amongst the working–class Cypriots who visit these, do not inhibit common interests in Britain. However, the evaluative/status distinctions made by Cypriots are often idioms for the expression of both political and objective class divisions and are brought into pay differentially according to the politico–economic context and the intersubjective element involved – they are neither consistently expressed nor permanently salient.

Concerning more objective class divisions, we can single out few strata. Firstly, there is a technocratic/professional group which is fairly small and composed of embassy officials, professionals and a diverse number of intellectuals. Those who function most as 'ethnic' have been brought over specifically by the High Commission to fill certain official posts or are doctors, accountants, solicitors and architects who are most dependent on an ethnic clientele. Some of this group will be economically and politically allied to the middle class either through origins or through their professional capacity. This group is not easily encompassed within a traditional class framework but it can be singled out in terms of possessing conditions of existence that identify it with a professional/ managerial/ intellectual stratum. There is no common consciousness however attributable to this group and a constituent of it will tend to ally its interests with social–democratic forces, populism and indeed socialism.

Secondly, there is a small group of large–scale businessmen who in terms of Marxist theory would be members of the capitalist class – these are concentrated in the large clothing or retail sectors. Most of them started off as small factory owners with peasant backgrounds and were strongly linked to the Greek–Cypriot community in terms of providing financial and other help for particular causes. They have since become more organisationally isolated although still largely depending on an ethnic labour input – their output being directed to British society however.

A third group that may be distinguished comprises the small factory or shop owner who is self–employed either using unpaid female labour or paid cheap female labour although usually also employing a small number of male Cypriot workers. Finally, the largest group comprises the waged–worker who is objectively economically different from the small scale capitalist but who is often subjectively non– distinguishable because of the degree of mobility there exists between the two groups and the orientations of male Cypriots towards self–employment. These strata do not have any necessary political objectives. In terms of Cypriot political divisions, the small factory/shop owner and the waged worker will tend to support the left, the others will tend to support the centre or the right. In terms of British political life there will be a tendency for all groups – apart from isolated segments – to vote for the Labour Party. Anomalies may exist between support in Cyprus and Britain, partly related to the ideological ambiguities in those who support the right wing Rally Party in Cyprus (often in terms of traditional nationalist allegiances and political solutions to the Cyprus problem) and the support for the British Labour Party as more sympathetic to the Cyprus cause.

However, in terms of numbers, the majority of Cypriots are to be found either as small self–employed or employees. The class division between employer and employee is blurred and the failure of Cypriot employees to organise into Trade Unions or to oppose their employers is largely a result of relating to them on ethnic and communal lines as opposed to class or conflict lines. This is different to Cyprus, where syndicalism is strong (especially left syndicalism within PEO – the Pancyprian Federation of Labour).

Ethnic Organisation and the Question of Class

In London, in particular, ethnic organisation involves political struggle around (a) issues of Cyprus – fought separately by different political colourings and (b) struggle that is directed towards the British state. However, where these ethnic lines coincide with class lines and the interests of the ethnic subject can be identified in class terms ethnic organisation may have an unintended class role. Its class role, however, is incipient and is brought into play differentially.

Ethnic organisation expresses a commonality of interests within the ethnic category. In AKEL, for example, employers and employees work together for a 'just' solution to the Cyprus problem. Issues which might divide the ethnic category, such as discussing what the implications of party members being employers, have not been adequately raised.

However, in other ways, ethnic organisation provides a forum for managing the effects of minority status and exclusion processes. It provides facilities for association, affiliation and contacts which help in employment, housing and economic advancement. Ethnicity provides symbols which facilitate a cohesion of interests – family and fictive kin, village networks and cultural idioms which foster differentiation from other groupings. Ethnicity also provides a basis for recruitment to work as is the case in Clothing and Catering within the Cypriot ethnic economy.

In British society, ethnic groups are usually migrant groups and they are in a disadvantaged position. Such groups, Black or White, are usually defined as outside the legitimate boundaries of the national collectivity, whether they are formally excluded in political/legal terms or not. They have thus had to take their ethnicity into account when attempting to manage the structures of ethnic disadvantage that they face. They have often used their ethnicity to advance their economic position in the society of residence. For example, Greek–Cypriots found that when the entered self–employment (out of a position of disadvantage) that it was in their interests to maintain control over certain sectors (e.g. clothing) and could use ethnic means (tie, resources) to survive effectively. To do this involved the exploitation of other Greek–Cypriots and especially female labour. So while a group of Greek–Cypriot men have successfully achieved the economistic aims of migration they have done so often through the use of Greek–Cypriot women. Greek–Cypriots may forego leisure and often pleasure in the pursuit of economistic ends and some have experienced cultural and personal impoverishment in so doing.

In addition to relying on ethnic labour, Greek–Cypriots can often rely on an ethnic clientele as is the case for shops, cafes and restaurants although the latter draw on a wider middle–class clientele given the popularity of Greek food. As for Asians and Italians, Cypriot food can become the basis of small shops and restaurants. Thus it is not merely a question of support being given through ethnic identification. Cypriots possess the resources and skills which are desired within the ethnic group. This provision, however, serves to reinforce the ethnic identification.

In the case of working for an ethnic employer it may not be so much that it is preferred because of ethnic identification but because there is exclusion from other work. This is especially true for women who have language difficulties, lack skills, educational qualifications and work-experience.

The maintenance of ethnic culture can go alongside both a structural inclusion in mainstream society and also be a useful political or personal/political resource. There is no necessary link between ethnic identity and structural inclusion/exclusion. But it is clear that where economic interests are being served then to preserve both the cultural and structural expression of separatism is instrumental.

However, there are class distinctions that need to be taken into account in assessing ethnicity which in fact refers to different processes for different socio-economic groups. The migrant who came over with no economic/educational resources uses ethnicity as a resource in its total sense. It is his/her world and is instrumental in his/her day-to-day material existence. The middle classes on the other hand possess a more universal resource (middle-class values, culture, education, rational discourse). Working class culture is context-related and is differentiated i.e. is ethnically, geographically and community based and specific. It is far easier for the middle-class Greek-Cypriot to function as a non-ethnic subject in his/her day-to-day life. He/she can choose to maintain the value of ethnic culture and identity and indeed may use this differentially according to the context – the case of identity-shifts is more common here than for the working class. The latter cannot choose to discard their ethnic constituent for as Gans has noted ethnicity is a largely working-class style. The propagation of ethnic and nationalist ideologies on the other hand is articulated by intellectuals and the intelligentsia.

The ethnic orientation of Greek-Cypriots, their home orientation and their social relations within the ethnic community does not deny them a position in the class structure of British society, for this latter must be conceptualised in terms of their role within the productive process. What is the extent of political mobilisation over class or ethnic interests, and the extent to which the latter obfuscate class relations or promote them?

We find in the case of Cypriots a contradiction. Their ethnicity makes them aware of the divisive nature of British society and the distinction between classes – as does their heritage of political and class consciousness in Cyprus. Their general support for Labour Party candidates, their identification with leftist politics in Cyprus and their representative bodies is confirmation of this. However, the ethnic orientation prevents them from taking an active part in British political life since Britain is a foreign country in which they have only 'temporarily' settled. It also prevents them from forming bonds with British workers or other immigrant workers. Literature in this field has supported the view that it is unlikely that migrants will act in class unison for no unity exists in political consciousness, material conditions or historical heritage of struggle. (Phizacklea and Miles, 1980)

For Greek-Cypriots ethnic identification prevents the formation of class consciousness within their work-situation. Many Cypriots work for Cypriot employers who have the same background as themselves and may be co-villagers or even kin. This identification as well as the hope that they too can achieve their aspirations and become employers, prevents them from forming a conception of class within the work-situation where it is generally most likely to develop.

8 Conclusion

The Greek-Cypriot experience in British society has been one whereby ethnicity has been used as a resource for achieving the economistic aims of migration. This ethnicity is not coterminous with that which Greek-Cypriots have in Cyprus since it is structured by the migration process and in relation to ethnic minority exclusions and subordinations. However, the economic and political conditions in Cyprus in the post war period have formed the initial bedrock for the changes and adaptations made. The strong sense of ethnic distinctiveness and the importance of Greek language and the family were constructions that predate the migrant experience but the ways in which they are expressed and their role has changed in the new setting of British society. This may in part explain why these facets of culture have not evolved naturally as they have in Cyprus but have stayed in a kind of 'time warp'. For example the Cypriot dialect that first generation migrants pass on to their children's is now only spoken in Cyprus in remote rural areas. The degree to which Cypriot parents in Britain espouse traditional norms of female sexual purity is also not found in urban Cyprus.

Greek Cypriots migrated to Britain for economic reasons and see their stay as instrumental in achieving a better standard of living for themselves and their children. Unlike a number of other migrant groups, Cypriots did not expect to be welcomed with open arms. Their experience of the national liberation struggle against the British during the EOKA period of 1955–1959 gave them a sense of familiarity but estrangement from the Colonial power.

Greek-Cypriots came to Britain expecting to work hard and had a will to succeed. Self-employment was a path that a significant number took. Some were indeed successful in achieving their economic aims although frequently at the expense of personal life and leisure. A significant proportion of the rest worked for Cypriot employers. A situation developed whereby migrants were employing migrants in order to achieve their economistic aims in a naturally difficult sphere (the small concerns and vulnerability of the clothing and catering sectors).

For employees, ethnic employment gave them opportunities they were excluded from otherwise through lack of language and low educational qualifications. Employers used ethnic and family ties in the process of self advancement. Women were the mainstay of this advancement (it was their labour that facilitated the ethnic economy). On the other hand, women too migrated for economic reasons, to work for themselves and for their families. The conditions of wage labour in Britain have not led, in an unambiguous fashion, to their economic independence. However, the British born Cypriot woman of the second or third generation has greater opportunities than her mother for emancipation as she learns to manage the cultural and sexual contradictions she faces.

Greek Cypriot economic placement is probably more typical than the race and ethnic literature in Britain indicates. Such literature tends to generalise from a specific type of experience, that of African Caribbeans. Asians, the Chinese, the Italians and the Jews in Britain have all tended to take the avenue to self-employment in catering and clothing. The Japanese in America, the Macedonians in Toronto and the Greeks in Australia are other cases in point. The role of such small scale enterprise is a focus of interest in much work on the informal economy (South 1080). The role of ethnic minorities is crucial here.

In terms of general points, the importance of studying the intersection of ethnic, class and gender processes in concrete cases is evident. However, some similarities may be noted amongst ethnic groups in the ways these might intersect. Firstly, migrant populations in terms of labour performed a useful function as replacement labour in the British economy at a particular stage of capitalist development when it was experiencing an economic boom. Subsequently, they provided pools of cheap labour for certain sectors. This is especially true for migrant women. The ethnicity, the economic insecurity and the patriarchal relations women experience will often although not always militate against trade union organisation. African Caribbean women have a greater tendency to organisation than other migrant women. This may be the result primarily of the specific sectors that they find employment in.

Secondly, the eventual economic adaptation of a migrant group will also depend on their particular class characteristics and gender and familial arrangements. The form of migrant labour will depend on the opportunities for the incorporation of skills, aptitudes and choices of migrants in interplay with the structural exclusions they face. These skills, aptitudes, choices and orientations do not remain fixed but are transformed under the new economic and social conditions. Cypriot entrepreneurship can be explained in this way.

The conditions for the sale of female labour are important, especially where the unit of migration is the family. Women are a source of cheap or unpaid labour and the patriarchal relations of the family may extend to those of work. Migrant women are less likely to see their work in the context of the liberation from domestic labour and more in the context of the economistic aims of migration of the family unit. However, the actual performance of wage labour can have contradictory and progressive effects as far as the emancipation of migrant women from the economic and social dependence on men and the family is concerned.

It is important to consider the interaction between the economic and political conditions of the country of origin and those of the country of migration. The country of origin may act as both a reference point and as a material structure within which ethnic subjects are still located. In the case of Cypriots there is a strong homeland orientation and a tendency towards economic investment in Cyprus. Economic and social processes in Cyprus are themselves affected by the character of the Greek Cypriot community in Britain. Remittances, property investment and consequently lop sided economic development in Cyprus, tourism and a cash nexus or moneymaking ethic, are cases in point. The implications are that migrant groups have to be seen as inserted within a total system of social relations encompassing the country of origin, the ethnic ecological base (and its ethnic, political and economic structures and networks) and the country of residence. Different migrant groups will present their own particular interconnections here.

Migrant populations often present a threat to the dominant ethnic group since they may be willing to subject themselves to worse conditions of employment and longer hours given their subordinate and dependent status. They may also be in competition with indigenous fractions of capital and unregulated by the British state if they work in the informal or hidden economy. This threat will tend to come to the fore and be expressed in different forms of ethnic and racist exclusions such as xenophobia, sectarianism or racism. These can all be regarded as forms of exclusionary nationalism which constitute the migrant as outside the legitimate boundaries of the national collectivity. This becomes exacerbated in times of economic recession and high competition for the resources of jobs and housing and access to state provision. Ethnic minority groups who remove themselves effectively from the mainstream, either economically or politically, are least likely to be affected by practices of exclusion and disadvantage. Anti muslim racism has grown precisely when Fundamentalist groups via the Rushdie affair appeared to challenge mainstream Western dominant cultural values. Therefore groups that are highly visible through the development of symbolic significance and negative meaning to cultural, religious, physical or other boundary markers, will be most affected. Such significance is constructed historically and contextually. Racist ideology can be regarded as a specific and extreme case of such a phenomenon.

As regards the salience of the ethnic category, this is facilitated by geographical and job segregation or concentration, a shared economic and class position, the existence of sexual exclusiveness to the group, the formation of social, political or ethnic organisations and the development of a distinct economic adaptation and orientation. These factors allow the ethnic dimension to appear as manifestly salient (because of a coincidence of ethnic and class position) even though what is often expressed is an articulation of ethnic, community, class and gender characteristics.

Ethnicity can function in different ways as a resource for different economic classes. Its economic importance is greater for those who lack skills and the cultural capital valued by the society of migration. Working class migrants require ethnic organisations and ties for economic survival and the countering of exclusion and disadvantage. All social classes will make economic use of ethnic networks however, for work, housing or as a source of capital. Entrepreneurial groups will shift their allegiance depending on specific economic interests. In a migrant situation this allegiance is expressed through the use of the ethnic category as workers, clients or customers. They will use the social and economic networks provided by ethnicity and have an economic interest in maintaining their own ethnic identity. On the other hand, ethnic allegiance may facilitate extensive exploitation of their own ethnic work force whilst they avow a commonality of ethnic interests with it.

Professional groups and intellectuals (the new middle class) do not require ethnic identity in an instrumental way, unless to adhere to it will yield specific gains. Middle class culture has the capacity to homogenise and cultural capital transcends ethnic boundaries in a large number of contexts. Such groups may still identify at the psychological level but ethnicity ceases to be as relevant at the solidary or political level. Some literature has noted this as symbolic or expressive ethnicity. Identification may take a romantic or idealistic character. Educational certification usually ensures an adequate participation in the social structure unless it is mediated by extreme forms of exclusion such as racism. However, exclusion on the basis of foreignness is current in the higher echelons of the Civil Service. Professional groups who make use of their ethnic category for economic purposes may be those who draw upon an ethnic clientele, such as lawyers, doctors or accountants.

Ethnicity is therefore a material condition for the sale of labour in the sense that it provides a basis for inclusion or exclusion and involves the formation of particular political, economic and ideological relations. It cannot be reduced to class for its basis is not given by the realm of economic relations and locations. Its basis is given through specific historical, cultural and material processes related to notions of belongingness and collectivity via a construction of an origin or essence to the group (Anthias, 1990). The differentiating boundaries of ethnicity can be used by economically and politically dominant groups to exploit and subordinate others. Ethnic (and gender) differentiations have to be written into any analysis of the concrete mode of production and the determinate social formation and into any analysis of the state and political power (Anthias and Yuval Davis, 1989). The particular development of capitalism and of the nation state has only been possible in relation to the particular forms that ethnic and sexual divisions have taken in the modern era.

Appendix I

Although the book is not focused around them, I made forty–four case studies of individuals and examined their history, settlement and way of life in England in some detail. This helped to build a picture along with other data. They were in all cases individuals who were already known to me intimately either through family links or through my involvement within the Cypriot community. I chose them according to age, sex and occupational criteria attempting to gain a fairly representative sample. I provide a few details about them here. These case studies will form the basis of a further project and I note them here since they fed into the analysis in a general way. My analysis has not depended upon them in any systematic way.

Males

Name	Age	Occupation
Yiannis	50	Wimpy Bar Owner
Tony	26	Wimpy Bar manager
Chris	22	Painter and decorator
Lambros	48	Shoe Factory Owner
Antonis	28	Chef
Petros	50	Grocery Owner
Stavros	36	Manager – Steak House
Nick	17	Student
Pavlos	37	Dry–Cleaning Shop Owner
Christos	32	Restaurant Owner
Simeos	43	Presser
George	40	Fish–Shop Owner
Andreas	52	Restaurant Owner
Panikos	28	Civil Engineer
Minos	27	Computer Programmer
Dinos	56	Fish–Shop Owner
Hambis	24	Car Mechanic
Kypros	58	Journalist

Thomas	35	Systems Analyst
Loukas	37	Presser
Haris	25	Cutter
Stathis	56	Fish and Chip Shop Owner
Total	22	

Females

Name	Age	Occupation
Ellou	50	Machinist
Evtyhia	20	Clerk
Andry	18	Student
Eleni	49	Housewife and family worker
Androulla	26	Clerk
Pantelitsa	48	Machinist
Froso	36	Doctor
Dina	23	Student
Maria	20	Hairdresser
Soulla	26	Manager (Marks and Spencer)
Niki	31	Machinist
Rea	63	Finisher
Anna	64	Homeworker
Beba	38	Social Worker
Maro	31	Secretary
Lena	34	Machinist
Katia	31	Teacher
Lena	36	Homeworker
Chystalla	46	Machinist
Vasso	36	Family worker
Thekla	70	Family worker
Nina	50	Homeworker
Total	22	

Age distribution

Age-group	Male	Female
15–25	4	4
25–35	6	6
35–45	5	4
45–55	4	5
55 +	3	3
Total	22	22

Occupational distribution

	Male	Female
Self employed	9	0
Managerial	2	1
Professional and related	4	3
Clerical	0	3
Students	1	2
Clothing workers	3	9
Catering	1	0
Other manual or service workers	2	4

Place of Birth

Cyprus – Village	16
Cyprus – Town	10
England	18
Total	44

Date of Migration (or parents' migration)

Before 1955	19
After 1955	25
Total	44

143

Reasons for migration (or parents' migration)

Economic	38
For a better life	3
Other reasons	3
Total	44

Marriage

	Male	Female
Married	18	10
Single	3	7
Divorced	1	3
Widowed	0	2
Married to Cypriot	16	7
Other	2	3

Educational Qualifications

	Male	Female
Degree or equivalent (or studying for degree or equivalent)	5	5
Secondary Education	7	8
Secondary Education with GCEs	(3)	(3)
Left school at 11 (in Cyprus)	8	8
Technical Training	2	1
Total	22	22

Ethnic Identity

Greek–Cypriot	12
Cypriot	22
Greek	1
English	0
British Cypriot	5
Don't know	2
Total	42

Appendix II

The problems of Statistical Data Used

Collection of statistics on immigrants has been on–going although interest is mainly on Britain's black population. Little public or political interest is given to white immigrants or those entering on work permits since 1971. Emphasis is on statistics about black people (immigrants and their British born children) and this has confused even more the term migrant. Very often the term "ethnic" is used as an umbrella term for minorities – usually meaning black. In the Home Office statistics and those collected by the OPCS, birthplace is used as an indication of physical characteristics and ethnic origin. The category of New Commonwealth immigrants includes whites for two reasons:

(1) whites born overseas
(2) Mediterranean NCW

Collection of statistics often aims at monitoring migration and data on employment is quite detailed although this is not the case for health, education, housing and social services.

I have used data collected by the OPCS 1971 and 1981. Data from the 1991 Census was not available when going to press. One problem with Census reports is that of mis–enumeration. The full Census count suffers less from this than the sample censuses. The Economic Activity Tables in the 1971 census are arrived at from a 10% Sample Survey and they also suffer from sampling errors. Here Cypriots are counted as part of the wider category of European New Commonwealth, along with those from Malta, Gibraltar and Gozo. The 1981 Census does not include Economic Activity Tables and therefore the official data on Cypriot employment is very out of date. Other sources of data on ethnic minority employment are published in the Labour Force Surveys. However, there is no identification of a Cypriot category produced by these reports.

As regards locating ethnic groups and migrant categories, there are the Country of Birth Tables that do distinguish those born in Cyprus and those whose parents were born in Cyprus. The numbers given do not distinguish between Greek and Turkish Cypriots. In 1971, the G.L.C. tabulations on economic activity provide data on parents' country of birth (Cypriots are included under the category of Mediterranean New Commonwealth). The Census itself only indicates parents' country of birth within the broader category of the New Commonwealth. No analogous figures were available in the 1981 census.

I have also used data presented in a report on Ethnic Minorities in Haringey, Februay 1980 which is partly based on the National Dwelling and Housing Survey 1977. The main problem is the identification of Cypriots as this was not one of the ethnic groups identified. According to the Haringey report it seems likely that most Turkish Cypriots classified themselves as "Turkish" while Greek Cypriots opted for "Other", "White" or "Other Asian". The "Turkish" and "Other" groups were combined in the report to form a new group the "Cypriot". The report recognises that this cannot serve as a basis for estimating the number of Cypriots in Haringey but that the social characteristics of Cypriots can be approximated by this method. We have to view the data in this report with some caution therefore and it cannot be used to assert specific empirical points. It may however help, given the limitations of published statistics on Cypriots with indicating possible general characteristics.

Bibliography

Adams, T.W. and Cottrell, A.J. (1968), *Cyprus Between East and West*, The John Hopkins Press, Baltimore

Adams T.W. (1964), *US Army Area Handbook for Cyprus*, Washington Government Relations Office, Washington

Adams, T.W. (1971), *AKEL – The Communist Party of Cyprus*, Hoover Institution Press, California

Advisory Conciliation and Arbitration Service (1978), Report no.13, London

Afsher, H. (1969), 'Women and Reproduction in Iran' in Yuval–Davis N. and F. Anthias (eds),– *Women, Nation, State*, Macmillan, London

Allen, S. and Wolkowitt, C. (1987), *Homeworking*, Macmillan, London

AKEL – Central Committee (1962), *10th Party Conference Papers*, Nicosia (in Greek)

AKEL – (1976), *50 years of AKEL*, Nicosia, Cyprus (in Greek)

Althusser, L. (1971), *ISA in Lenin & Philosophy and other essays*, New Left Books, London

Amos, V. and Parmar, P. (1984), 'Challenging Imperial Feminism', *Feminist Review* no.17

Anthias, T. (1941), Living Cyprus – Essays in Folk–lore, Nicosia Cyprus (in Greek)

Anthias, F. and Ayres, R. (1979), Nationalism and Socialism in Cyprus *CSE Conference Papers*, London

Anthias, F. (1980), 'Women and the Reserve Army of Labour', *Capital and Class*, no.10

Anthias, F. (1982), Ethnicity and Class among Greek Cypriot migrants – a study in the conceptualisation of ethnicity, *Ph.D. Thesis University of London*

Anthias, F. (1983), 'Sexual Divisions and Ethnic Adaptation – Greek–Cypriot women in Britain', in Phizacklea A. (ed) (1983), *One Way Ticket*, Routledge, London

Anthias, F. and Yuval–Davis, N. (1983), 'Contextualising Feminism–ethnic gender and class divisions' in *Feminist Review*, no.15

Anthias, F. and Yuval–Davis, N. (1989), 'Introduction', in Yuval–Davis and Anthias (eds) *Woman, Nation, State*, Macmillan, London

147

Anthias, F. (1989), 'Women and Nationalism in Cyprus' in Yuval–Davis and Anthias (eds.) *Women, Nation, State*, Macmillan, London

Anthias, F. (1990), 'Race and Class Revisited – Conceptualising Race and Racisms', *Sociological Review*, Vol. 38, No.1, February

Anthias, F. (1991), 'Gendered Ethnicities in the British Labour Market', *paper presented to International conference on Migration*, Berlin May 13–14th

Anthias, F. and Ayres, R. (1983),'Ethnicity and Class in Cyprus', *Race and Class*, Vol. 25, No.1, Summer

Anthias, F. and Yuval–Davis, N. (1992), *Racialised boundaries, Racism and the Community*, Routledge, London

Ardill, N. and Cross, N. (1987), *Undocumented Lives – Britain's Unauthorised Migrant Workers*, Runnymede Trust, London

Art and Work, (1980), Published by Theatre Technic, London

Attalides, M. (ed) (1977a), *Cyprus Reviewed*, Cyprus Social Research Centre, Nicosia, Cyprus

Attalides, M. (1979), Cyprus: *Nationalism and Interactional Politics* Q Press, Edinburgh

Attalides, M. (1977), 'Forms of peasant incorporation in Cyprus during the Last Century' in E. Gellner and J. Waterbury, *Patrons and Clients*, Duckworth, (1977b), London

Ballard, C. (1979), Conflict Continuity and change in V. Saifullah Khan *Minority Families in Britain*, The MacMillan Press, London and Basingstoke

Ballard, R. and Ballard, C. (1977), 'The Sikhs: the development of South in Britain' in Watson, J.L. (ed) *Between Two Cultures*, Blackwell, Oxford

Banton, M. (1959), *White and Coloured The Behaviour of British People towards Coloured Immigrants*, Jonathan Cape, London

Barker, M. (1981), *The New Racism*, Junction Books, London

Barron, R.D. and Norris G.M. (1976), 'Sexual Divisions and the Dual Labour Market' in D. Barker and S. Alle (eds) *Dependence and Exploitation in Work and Marriage*, Longman, London and New York

Barth, F. (1969), *Ethnic Groups and Boundaries*, Allen & Unwin, London

Beckingham, C.P. (1957), 'Islam and Turkish Nationalism in Cyprus' in *Die Welt des Islam*, 5: 65–83

Beechey, V. (1979), 'Women and Production: a critical analysis of some sociological theories of women's work' in A. Kuhn and A. Wolpe (eds) *Feminism and Materialism*, Routledge and Kegan Paul, London

Beechey, V. (1986), *Unequal Work*, Pluto Press, London

Bell, D. (1975), 'Ethnicity and social change' in N. Glazer and D.F. Moynihan (1979), *Ethnicity, theory, experience* Harvard University Press, Cambridge Mass and London

Ben–Tovim, G. et al, (1981), 'Race, Left–Strategies and the State' *Politics and Power* 3 Routledge and Kegan Paul, London

Blackburn, R. and Mann, M. (1979), *The Working Class in the Labour Market*, Macmillan, London

Blauner, R. (1969), 'Internal Colonialism and Ghetto Revolt', *Social Problems* vol. 16, no.4 Spring

du Boulay, J. (1974), *Portrait of a Greek Mountain Village*, Clarendon Press, Oxford

Bourne, J. and Sivanandan, A. (1980), 'Cheerleaders and Ombudsmen: the sociology of race relations in Britain' *Race and Class*, vol. XXI no.4

Brown, C. (1984), *Black and White Britain*, Heinemann, London

Brown, M. (1974), *Sweated Labour* Low Pay Unit Pamphlet no.1

Cacoyiannis, G. (1959), *The Leadership of AKEL and the Armed Struggle – A Marxist Critique*, Nicosia, Cyprus

Campbell, J.K. (1964), *Honour, family and Patronage, A study of Institutions and Moral Values in a Greek Mountain Community*, Clarendon, Oxford

Carchedi, G. (1975), 'On the Economic Identification of the New Middle Class', in *Economy and Society*, vol. 4, no. : 1–86

Carby, H. (1982), 'White Women Listen! Black Feminism and the Bundaries of Sisterhood' in Centre for Contemporary Cultural Studies, *The Empire Strikes Back*, Hutchinson, London

Castells, M. (1975), 'Immigrant Workers and Class Struggle in Advanced Capitalism' in *Politics and Society* vol. 5 no.1

Castles, S. and Kosack, G. (1972), 'The function of Labour Immigration in Western European Capitalism', *New Left Review* no.73

Castles, S. and Kosack, G. (1973), *Immigrant workers and Class Structure in Western Europe*, Oxford University Press, Oxford

Castles, S. *Here for Good*, Western Europe's New Ethnic Minorities, Pluto Press, London

Christophia, D. (1977), 'The importance of "peaceful co–existence" in contemporary society', *NEOS DEMOCRATIS* Nicosia, Cyprus March

Clough, E. and Quarmby, J. (1978), *A public library service for ethnic minorities in Great Britain*, The Library Association, London

Cohen, A. (1969a), *Custom and Politics in Urban Africa*, Routledge and Kegan Paul, London

Cohen, A. (1969b), 'Political Anthropology: the analysis of the Symbolism of power relations' in *Man* 4: 217–35

Cohen, A. (1974), *Urban Ethnicity*, Tavistock, London

Cohen, P. (1988), 'The Perversions of Inheritance' in Cohen, P. and Bains, H.S., *Multi–racist Britain*, Macmillan, London

Cohen, P. and Bains, H. (eds) *Multi–Racist Britain*, Macmillan, London

Commission for Industrial Relations, (1974), Report no.77, *Clothing Wages Councils*, April 25th

Commission for Racial Equality, (1979), *Ethnic Minorities in Britain*, London

Constantinides, P. (1977), 'The Greek Cypriots: Factors in the Maintenance of Ethnic Identity' in J. Watson (ed) (1977), *Between Two Cultures* Blackwell, Oxford

van Coufoudakis (ed), (1976), *Essays on the Cyprus Conflict*, Pella Publishing Company, New York

Cox, O. (1970), *Caste, Class and Race: A Study in Social Dynamics*, Modern Reader Paperbacks, New York

Coyle, A. (1982), 'Sex and Skill in the Organisation of the Clothing Industry', in J. West (ed) *Work, Women and the Labour Market*, Routledge and Kegan Paul, London

Craft, N. and Craft, A. (1981), *The participation of Ethnic Minorities in Further and Higher Education*, Nuffield Foundation Study, Oxford

Crine, S. (1979), *The Hidden Army*, Low Pay Unit, London

Crine, S. (1981), *The Pay and conditions of Homeworkers*, submission to The House of Commons Select Committee on Employment, Low Pay Unit, February, London

Crouzet, F. (1973), *Le Conflit de Chypre* 1946–1959 2 vols, Brussels, Establishments Emile Bruylant

Cyprus Pocket Handbook, (1956), *Containing Indisputable Evidence of the 78 years of Colonial Exploitation of the people of Cyprus*, Athens

Cyprus Social Research Centre, (1975), *Cypriot Women, Rise and Downfall*, Public Information Office, Nicosia

Dahya, B. (1974), 'The Nature of Pakistani Ethnicity in Industrial Cities in Britain', in Cohen, A. *Urban Ethnicity*, Tavistock, London

Davis, J. (1977), *People of the Mediterranean*, Routledge and Kegan Paul

Davis, N.Y. (1981), 'Women as Reproducers of National Collectivities', Paper presented to History Workshop, London November

Demetriades, E.I. and Psacharopoulas, G. (1979), 'Education and pay structure in Cyprus', *International Labour Review*, vol. 118, no.1 January–February

Dench, G. (1975), *Maltese in London: A Case Study in the Erosion of Ethnic Consciousness*, Routledge and Kegan Paul, London

Doeringer, P.B. and Piore, M.J. (1971), *Internal Labour Markets and Manpower Analysis*, Lexington, Mass.

Edwards, R.C., Reich, M. and Gordon, D. (1975), *Labour Market Segmentation*, D.C: Heath and Co., Lexington, Mass.

Eggleston, J. (1983), *Education for Some*, Trentham Books, Trentham

Elliott, P. (1981), *Library Needs of Mother–Tongue Schools in London* Research Report no.6, School of Librarianship, The Polytechnic of North London

Ethnic Minorities in Haringey, (Feb. 1980),London Borough of Haringey Corporate Planning Unit

Gabriel, J. and Ben–Tovim, G. (1978), 'Marxism and the Concept of Racism' in *Economy and Society* vol. 7, no.2, May

Gaitskell, D. and Unterhalter, E. (1989), 'Mothers of the nation: a comparative analysis of nation, race and motherhood in Africaner nationalism and the African National Congress; in N. Yuval Davis and F. Anthias (eds.), *Woman, Nation, State*, Macmillan, London

Gans, H.J. (1979), 'Symbolic Ethnicity: the future of ethnic groups and cultures in America', *Ethnic and Racial Studies*, vol. 2, no.1, January

Gellner, E. (1983), *Nations and Nationalism*, Blackwell, Oxford

Gellner, E. (1987), *Culture, Politics and Identity*, Cambridge University Press, Cambridge

Gellner, E. (1964), *Thought and Change*, Weidenfeld and Nicolson, London

Gellner, E. and Waterbury, J. (eds), (1977), *Patrons and Clients*, Duckworth, London

Genovese, E.D. (1968), *In Red and Black: Marxist Explorations in Southern and Afro-American History* Random House, New York

Genovese, E.D. (1974), *Roll Jordan Roll: The World the Slaves made*, Andre Deutch, London

George, V. and Millerson, G. (1967), 'The Cypriot Community in London', *Race 8*, : 277–92

Georgiou, A. (1981), 'Cypriot Women in Politics', *Equal Rights, Equal Duties Conference*, Nicosia (in Greek)

Gilmore, D. (1977), 'Patronage and Class Conflict in Southern Spain' *Man* XII 3/4 : 446–58

Gilroy, P. (1980), 'Managing the "underclass": a further note on the sociology of race relations in Britain', *Race and Class* XXII, I

Gilroy, P. (1987), *There Aint no Black in the Union Jack*, Hutchinson, London

Glazer, N. and Moynihan, D.P. (1965), *Beyond the Melting Pot*, MIT Press, Mass.

Glazer, N. and Moynihan, D.P. (1975), *Ethnicity, Theory and Experience*, Harvard University Press, Cambridge Mass and London

Glazer, N. (1981), 'The Ethnic Factor', *Encounter* July : 7

Gordon, M. (1978), *Human Nature, class and ethnicity*, Oxford University Press, New York

Gordon, M. (1964), *Assimilation in American Life*, Oxford University Press, New York

Gordon, P. and Newnham, A. (1986), *Different Worlds*, Runneymede Trust, London

Gouldner, A. (1979), *The future of the Intellectuals and the rise of the new class*, MacMillan, London

Government Census Report for Cyprus (1946)

Grivas, G. (1964), *Guerrilla Warfare and EOKA's Struggle*, Longmans, London

Guillaumin, C. (1988), 'Race and Nature: the System of Marks', *Feminist Issues*, Fall

Hall, S. (1980), 'Race, articulation and societies structured in dominance in UNESCO', *Sociological Theories: Race and Colonialism*, Paris

Hall, S. (1988), 'New Times', *Marxism Today*

Hall, S. (1989), 'New Ethnicities', *Black Film, Black Cinema*, ICA Documents 7, London

Hall, S., Critcher, C., Jefferson, T., Clarke, J., Roberts, B., (1978), *Policing the Crisis: Mugging, the State and Law and Order* The Macmillan Press, London

Haringey Area Management Team Report on Homeworking in Haringey, (March 1980)

Haringey Area Management Team (1981), Homeworking: *Progress Reports and Recommendations*, The Borough of Haringey, April

Haringey Area Management Team (1981), Report (24th March) *West Green Childcare Survey Summary*

Haringey Employment Project (1980), *The Clothing Industry in the Cypriot Community*

Hartmann, H. (1979), 'Marxism and Feminism, towards a more progressive union', *Capital and Class*, no.8

Hechter, M. (1975), *Internal Colonialism*, Routledge and Kegan Paul, London

Hechter, M. (1987), 'Nationalism as group solidarity', *Ethnic and Racial Studies*, vol. 10. no.4, October

Hill, G. (1952), *A History of Cyprus* vol. 4 Cambridge University Press

Hirst, P. (1976), 'Althusser and the Theory of Ideology', *Economy and Society*, no.5, : 385–412

Hoel, B. (1982), 'Contemporary Clothing Sweatshops, Asian Female Labour and Collective Organisation', in J. West (ed) *Work, Women and the Labour Market*, Routledge and Kegan Paul, London

Hope, E. Kennedy, M. and de Winter, A. (1976), 'Homeworkers in North London' in D.L. Barker and S. Allen *Dependence and Exploitation in Work and Marriage*, Longman, London

Horton, J. (1965), 'Order and Conflict Models as Competing Ideologies for the Study of Race' in *American Journal of Sociology* pp.708–725

House, W.J. (1980), *Labour Market Segmentation and Sex Discrimination in Cyprus*, Statistics and Research Department Ministry of Finance, Nicosia, Cyprus

Hunter, A. (1981), 'In the Wings–New Right Organisation and Ideology', *Radical America*, vol. 15, Nos.1 & 2: 113–140, Spring

Ifeka, C. (1977), Correspondence *MAN* N.S. 10: 5

Jeffery, P. (1976), *Migrants and Refugees: Muslim and Christian Pakistani Families in Bristol*, Cambridge University Press, Cambridge

Jenness, L. (1962), *The Economics of Cyprus* McGill University Press, Montreal

Jones, C. (1977), *Immigration and Social Policy in Britain*, Tavistock Publications, London

Kahn, J. (1981), 'Explaining Ethnicity', in *Critique of Anthropogy*, vol. 4, no.16, Spring : 43–53

Khan, V.S. (1977), 'The Pakistanis: Mirpuri villagers at home and in Bradford' in J. Watson (ed) *Between Two Cultures*, Blackwell, Oxford

Khan, V.S. (ed) (1979), *Minority Families in Britain: Support and Stress*, The MacMillan Press, London and Basingstoke

Kandiyoti, D. (1988), 'The Patriarchal Bargain', *Gender and Society*

Killian, L. (1980), 'Concentration and Organisation as Factors in Mobilisation for Ethnic Conflict' Unpublished paper 25.11.80

Kitromilides, P. (1977), 'From Co-existence to Confrontation, The Dynamics of Ethnic Conflict in Cyprus' in M. Attalides (1977), *Cyprus Reviewed* Social Research Centre, Nicosia, : 35–69

Kyrris, C.P. (1977), *Peaceful Co-existence in Cyprus under British rule (1878–1959) and after independence*, Nicosia, Cyprus

Ladbury, S. (1977), 'The Turkish Cypriots: Ethnic Relations in London and Cyprus' in J. Watson (ed) *Between Two Cultures*, Blackwell, Oxford

Ladbury, S. (1979), *Turkish Cypriots in London: economy, society, culture and change*, Ph.D. Thesis, S.O.A.S. University of London

Leewenberg, (1979), *The Cypriots in Haringey* Research Report no.1 School of Librarianship The Polytechnic of North London

Lenin, V.I. (1968), *The National Question Collected Works* vol. 19, Lawrence and Wishart, London

Lenin, V. (1916), 'Critical remarks on the national question' in *Collected Works of Lenin*, Forign Languages Publishing House, Moscow

Liasides, P. (1979), *Nekatomenoi Aeries* Ministry of Education, Nicosia Cyprus (in Greek)

Li Causi, L. (1975), 'Anthropology and Ideology', *Critique of Anthropology* : 4-5, 90-109

Light, I.H. (1972), *Ethnic Enterprise in America: Business and Welfare among Chinese, Japanese and blacks*, Berkeley, California

Littlewood, P, (1980), 'Patronage Ideology and Reproduction', *Critique of Anthropology* Spring

Loizos, P. (1976), 'Changes in Property Transfers among Greek-Cypriot Villagers', *MAN N.S 10*, : 503-523

Loizes, P. (1977), 'Politics and patronage in a Cypriot village 1920-1970' in E. Gellner and J. Waterbury *Patrons and Clients*, Duckworth, London

Lowy, M. (1976), 'Marxists and the National Question', *New Left Review* no. 96: 83

Luke, H. (1957), *Cyprus, a Portrait and an Appreciation*, George C. Harrap, London

Lyon, M. (1972), 'Race and Ethnicity in pluralistic societies', *New Community* vol. 1 no.4, Summer

Markides, K.C. (1977), *The Rise and Fall of the Cyprus Republic*, Yale University Press, Newhaven and London

Markides, K., Nikito, E. and Rangan, E. (1978) *LYSI - Social Change in a Cypriot Village*, Social Research Centre, Nicosia Cyprus

Marx, K. (1976), *Capital* vol.1, Penguin, Harmondsworth

Marx, K. (1970), *Manifesto of the Communist Party*, Foreign Languages Press, Peking

Mayhew, K. and Rosewell, B. (1978), 'Immigrants and occupational crowding in Great Britain', *Oxford Bulletin of Economics and Statistics* vol. 40, no.3

Meek, R.L. (1971), *Marx and Engels on the population Bomb*, Ramparts Press, California

MEMORIAL 1929, (1929), *A memorial dealing with the chief grievances of the People of Cyprus*, (presented by the Greek members of the Legislative Council to the Secretary of State for the Colonies at Downing Street), signed 20th July at Nicosia

Meyer, A.J. and Vassiliou S. (1962), *The Economy of Cyprus*, Harvard University Press

Miles, R. (1980), 'Class, race and ethnicity: a critique of Cox's theory', *Ethnic and Racial Studies*, vol. 3, no.2

Minority Rights Group, (1978), *Western Europe's Migrant Workers*, Report no.28, London

Mortimore, P. (1981), 'Achievement in Schools' ILEA *Contact* 13th November, London

Nairn, T. (1977), *The Breakup of Britain*, New Left Books, London

Nearchou, V. (1960), 'The Assimilation of the Cypriot Community in London' MA Thesis, University of Birmingham

NEOS ANTHROPOS, (1962), Newspaper of the Communist Party of Cyprus (KKK) Cyprus, January 1926

NUTGW, (1982), 'A plea to all clothing workers', *Parikiaki Haravgi*, March, London

Oakley, R. (ed), (1968), *New Backgrounds: The Immigrant Child at Home and at School*, Oxford University Press (for the Institute of Race Relations)

Oakley, R. (1970), 'Cypriots in Britain', *Race Today*, April

Oakley, R. (1971), 'Cypriot Migration and Settlement in Britain', D.Phil, University of Oxford

Oakley, R. (1979), 'Family Kinship and Patronage' in V. Saifullah Khan (1979) *Minority Families in Britain*, The Macmillan Press, London

Oakley, R. (1982), Review: in *Times Higher Education Supplement*, March

OPCS, (1971), Office of Population Censuses and Statistic *Census*, HMSO, London

OPCS (1974), Census 1971, *Small Area Tabulation*, HMSO, London

Orr, C.W. (1918), *Cyprus under British Rule*, Robert Scott, London

Papadopoulos, (1965), *Social and Historical Data on Population 1570–1881*, Cyprus Research Centre, Nicosia

Parikiaki Haravgi, Weekly newspaper of AKEL in London

Parkin, F. (1979), *The Marxist Theory of Class, a bourgeois critique*, Tavistock Publications, London

Parks, R.E. (1950), *Race and Culture*, Free Press, Glencoe, Illinois

Patterson, O. (1977), *Ethnic Chauvinism: The Reactionary Impulse*, Stein and Day, New York

Patterson, S. (1965), *Dark Strangers, A Study of West Indians in London*, Harmondsworth Penguin abridged ed. 1965

Peach, C. (1968), *West Indian Migration to Britain*, Oxford University Press, Oxford

Peristiany, (ed) (1966), 'Honour and Shame in a Cypriot Highland Village' in *Honour and Shame, the Value of Mediterranean Society*, University of Chicago Press

Persianis, P.K. (1971), *The political and Economic factors as the main determinants of education policy in independent Cyprus 1960–70*, Ph.D Thesis, London University

Phizacklea, A. and Miles, R. (1980), *Labour and Racism*, Routledge and Kegan Paul, London

154

Pollis, A. (1966), 'Political Implications of the Modern Greek Concept of Self', British Journal of Sociology 16

Pollis, A. (1973), 'Intergroup Conflict and British Colonial Policy: The Case of Cyprus', *Comparative Politics* vol. 5, July

Poulantzas, N. (1975), *Classes in Contemporary Capitalism*, New Left Books, London

Poulantzas, N. (1978), 'The New Petty Bourgeoisie' in A. Hunt (ed) *Class and Class Structure*, Lawrence and Wishart, London

Public Information Office, (1959), *CYPRUS – The problem in perspective*, Nicosia, Cyprus

Public Information Office, (1974), *Economic Consequences of the Turkish Invasion*, Nicosia, Cyprus

Public Information Office, (1977), *Expulsions of Greek–Cypriots*, Nicosia, Cyprus

Republic of Cyprus Statistics and Research Dept. Ministry of Finance, (1977–78), *Cypriot Students Abroad*, Nicosia, Cyprus

Republic of Cyprus Statistics and Research Dept, Ministry of Finance, (1979), Manpower Survey *14th Manpower Survey*, Nicosia, Cyprus

Republic of Cyprus Statistics and Research Dept, Ministry of Finance, (1977), *Statistics of Wages, Salaries and Hours of Work* Nicosia, Cyprus

Rex, J. and Moore, R. (1967), *Race, Community and Conflict, A Study of Sparkbrook*, Oxford University Press for IRR, London

Rex, J. (1970), *Race Relations in Sociological Theory*, Weidenfeld and Nicholson, London

Rex, J. and Tomlinson, S. (1979), *Colonial Immigrants in a British City*, Routledge and Kegan Paul, London

Rex, J. (1981), 'A working paradigm for race relations research'. *Ethnic and Racial Studies*, vol. 4 no.1, January

Rose, E.J.B.and Deakin, N. et al (1969), *Colour and Citizenship, A Report on British Race Relations*, Oxford University Press (for the Institute of Race Relations), Oxford

Saul, J.S. (1979), 'The dialectic of class and tribe', *Race and Class*, XX, 4

Savvides, (1978), 'Leninism and the Struggle to Democratise Society in Cyprus', *World Marxist Review*, June

Schlesinger, P. (1982), 'In Search of the intellectuals – some comments on recent theory', in *Media, Culture and Society*, vol. 4

Schnedier, J. (1971), 'Of Vigilance and Virgins', *Ethnography* 9

Shah, S. (1975), *Immigrants and Employment in the Clothing Industry*, Runnymede, London

Silverman, (1977), 'Patronage as Myth' in E. Gellner and J. Waterbury (1977) *Patrons and Clients*, Duckworth, London

Sivanandan, A. (1976), 'Race, Class and the State – in black experience in Britain', *Race and Class*, Vol. 25, No.2

Smith, A.D. (ed), (1976), *Nationalist Movements*, The Macmillan Press Ltd, London and Basingstoke

Smith, D.J. (1977), *Racial Disadvantage in Britain*, Penguin, Harmondsworth

Smith, D.J. (1981), *Unemployment and Racial Minorities*, Policy Studies Institute, London

South, N. (1980), *The Informal Economy and Local Labour Markets* SSRC Workshop – Research Initiatives on Local Labour Markets and the Informal Economy, Middlesex Polytechnic

Sparsis, (1980), 'Cypriot Women in Politics', *POGO Conference Papers* POGO, Nicosia, Cyprus (in Greek)

Storrs, R. (1945), *Orientations*, Nicholson and Watson, London

Surridge, B.J. (1930), *A Survey of Rural Life in Cyprus*, Nicosia, Cyprus

The Ecclesiastical Laws of the Cyprus Church, (1968), Introduced by K. Chrisostomides, Pygmalion Press, London

The Rampton Report, (1981), *West Indian Children in our schools*, Cmnd 8273 HMSO

The Runnymede Trust and the Radical Statistics Race Group, (1980), *Britain's Black Population*, Heinemann Educational Books, London

Taylor, D.M. and Giles, H. (1979), 'At the crossroads of Research into Language and Ethnic Relations' in H. Giles and B. Saint-Jacques *Language and Ethnic Relations*, Pergamon Press, New York

Trades Unions Congress, (1977), 'Homeworking', A TUC Statement, London

Van den Berghe, P.L. (1967), *Race and Racism*, John Wiley and Sons, New York

Wallman, S. (1978), 'The Boundaries of "Race": Process of Ethnicity in England', *Man* vol. 13 no.2, June

Wallman, S. (1979), *Ethnicity at Work*, Macmillan, London

Watson, J. (1977), *Between Two Cultures*, Blackwell, Oxford

Weber, M. (1969), *Economy and Society*, vol. 1, Bedminster Press, New York

Westergard, J. and Reisler, H. (1975), *Class in a Capitalist Society: A Study of Contemporary Britain*, Penguin, Harmondsworth

Williams, G. (1977), 'Class relations in a neo-colony The Case of Nigeria' in C.W. Gutland and P. Waterman (ed) (1977), *African Social Studies A Radical Reader*, Heinemann, London

Willis, P. (1977), *Leaning to Labour*, Saxon House, London

Windsow, P. (1964), 'NATO and the Cyprus Crisis', *Adelphi Papers* November :3

Wright, E.O. (1976), *Class Boundaries in Advanced Capitalist Societies*, New Left Review 98 : 3–41

Ziartides, A. (1980), 'Cypriot Women in Politics', *POGO Conference Papers* POGO Nicosia, Cyprus (in Greek)

Zubaida, S. (ed), (1970), *Race and Racialism*, Tavistock, London

Zubaida, S. (1977), 'Theories of Nationalism' in G. Littlejohn, B. Smart, J. Wakeford and N. Yuval-Davis (eds.) *Power and the State*, Croom Helm, London